MOHAWK MOUNTAIN SKI AREA

T0274087

MOHAWK MOUNTAIN SKI AREA

The Birth of Snowmaking

JAMES SHAY

Foreword by Carol Schoenknecht Lugar,
President of Mohawk Mountain

THE
History
PRESS

Published by The History Press
Charleston, SC
www.historypress.com

First published 2024

Manufactured in the United States

ISBN 9781467156646

Library of Congress Control Number: 2024941867

To Sharon, my lovely wife, and Sarah, my wonderful daughter.

And to all the people and friends who have worked and skied at Mohawk Mountain. Thanks to the snowmakers, groomers, ski patrollers, lift operators, rentals department crew, ski/snowboard instructors and the many other employees who make the Mohawk Mountain ski area a very cool place. Special thanks to Mohawk president Carol Lugar, daughter of the ski area's founders, and the Hedden family, who have kept Mohawk open for more than seventy-five years.

CONTENTS

FOREWORD

This book tells the story of a vision, as well as the incredible people who came together to create, to lead and to share a special place for snow lovers: Mohawk Mountain. Enjoy our story, and thank you for being a part of it.

Walt Schoenknecht was a dreamer and creator, imagineer, icon and, above all, a lover of snow. His gregarious and charismatic nature led so many into the world of skiing—as enthusiasts, avid supporters, investors and staff. His entrepreneurial ideas, often ahead of the times, led to significant industry advances and creative mountain development solutions, but his belief, and his overriding goal, was to ensure that everyone had fun in the snow.

Peg Schoenknecht was a thinker who made Walt's dreams a practical reality. As money and business manager, creative designer and pragmatic implementer, she embraced and supported Walt's dreams and found ways to see them through, with practicality and a healthy dose of realism. Peg's steadfast belief in Mohawk Mountain's future, and in Steve Hedden's and my ability as leaders, made it possible to move forward after the 1989 tornados. Her support, trust and advice were integral to our successful rebuilding and timely reopening. She continued to see us through more years of strengthening Mohawk Mountain as it evolved.

To Mom and Dad, special thanks for giving me (and my family) the best backyard ever. It's been the adventure of my lifetime to grow up in the ski industry and be part of its culture, history, future and legacy. From

The Schoenknechts out for a day of skiing at Mohawk Mountain in the early 1950s. *From left to right*: Walt, Peg and their daughter, Carol. *Mohawk Mountain ski area.*

on-the-ground business operations to ski trips around the world, you gave me the foundation of my knowledge. You taught me to be creative, face challenges, embrace change and enjoy great conditions, especially when we created them.

Steve Hedden is Mohawk Mountain's former vice-president and my trusted colleague. Our friendship was founded in childhood, and we grew into the best kind of business partners—open, innovative and confident. We shared ideas, talents, creativity and skills, all with mutual respect and pragmatic humor. We always found a way to work together. In the tornado's aftermath, we rebuilt an amazing, resilient and successful business despite challenges, and we did it in the face of those who said we couldn't. Now retired, Steve remains a significant part of the Mohawk Mountain group.

Don Hedden, Mohawk Mountain's vice-president, is our innovative and hardworking mountain master—talented, creative and forward-thinking. His expertise with snowmaking, grooming and lifts has taken Mohawk Mountain to the forefront of best conditions and mountain readiness. He also brings subtle wit and vision to our operations. He is a wonderful colleague and friend.

What we do as leaders can only be accomplished with a team of staff and advisors. Since our beginning, we've had generations of people working hard to create a special place and amazing experiences. It takes countless skills and talents to make Mohawk Mountain run. For some, it's a first job or the start of a career; for some, it's a way to stay busy or connect with others. Some just want to ski.

We also work with a dedicated group of professionals. Everyone shares so much of themselves, in their talent, vision and guidance and in their ideas and time. A capable and talented next generation will carry Mohawk Mountain forward. This energetic and enthusiastic team has great ideas, innovations and exciting visions for Mohawk Mountain's future operations and growth. Some are family and some have adopted us, but all are part of a trusted team. We can't wait to see what they accomplish.

Little of what we do can be achieved without the support of families and friends. They have put up with our long work hours, delayed dinners and missed events. They pitch in to help as needed and without being asked. They share (or at least tolerate) our love of winter. They are our foundation.

—Carol Schoenknecht Lugar

Carol Schoenknecht Lugar has been Mohawk Mountain's president since 1986, vice-president from 1968 to 1986 and lifetime apprentice. Born in Cornwall, Connecticut, and raised around Mohawk Mountain and Mount Snow, Vermont (with a few runs in other ski towns along the way), she has been an integral part of Mohawk Mountain's story and its legacy. While Mohawk Mountain has been a centerpiece in her life, there's also time for travel, gardens, home, crafts, books, friends and family.

ACKNOWLEDGEMENTS

There is a saying: "Journalism is the first rough draft of history." Who first coined the phrase is up for debate. Many attribute it to *Washington Post* president and publisher Philip L. Graham, who said it in a 1963 meeting with overseas correspondents. Others say that the phrase may have come from an unnamed editorial writer with the *Washington Post* in the 1940s. Regardless of who first said it, the phrase holds to be true.

Few of the people present when Mohawk first opened more than seventy-five years ago are alive today. Gone are Walt and Peg Schoenknecht, the founders of Mohawk. Also passed are the three Connecticut aviation engineers who created the first snowmaking machine used at the Mohawk ski area.

Walt and Peg's daughter, Carol Lugar, was there when Mohawk opened and the first snowmaking system was installed. But she was a young child then. Her recollections come from the stories her parents shared.

Fortunately, the work of former ski writers is more accessible thanks to research websites like newspapers.com, ancestry.com and Google News Archives. When I was in college, finding news articles was more difficult and time-consuming. First, it required finding a research book listing subjects, articles and publication dates. Then you had to get rolls of microfilm and search for the articles.

Much of my research came from the "first rough drafts of history" stories written decades ago. The newspaper articles also provide a glimpse of how modern skiing evolved and opened up the sport for everyone.

I want to thank the Cornwall Historical Society, especially its curator, Suzanne Fateh. The CHS was one of my first stops in doing research. As it turned out, the CHS was considering an exhibit on the Mohawk ski area. Thus, Suzanne and I had a shared mission to give Mohawk its rightful place in history. Early Mohawk photos are now digitized and preserved for future generations.

Initially, getting documents and photographs from Mohawk's first years was a challenge; it was believed that many were destroyed in the July 10, 1989 tornados. Fortunately, boxes of Mohawk news clippings, photos, brochures, posters and typewritten correspondences were found, uncovering a treasure-trove of memories.

I want to thank Mohawk president Carol Lugar, General Manager Dan Hedden and Steve Hedden, who were the keys in unlocking Mohawk's past. And thanks go to Ben Waller, a Cornwall resident, who shared memories of the tornados that ravaged the ski area.

Also, a thumbs-up to the New England Ski Museum in Franconia, New Hampshire, for photos of the first snowmaking machines and Walt's use of crushed ice on ski trails. The museum's Chronology of Snowmaking was especially helpful.

Finally, I want to thank my wife, Sharon, for her support, patience, guidance and editing.

INTRODUCTION

When you visit the Mohawk Mountain ski area in Cornwall, Connecticut, you won't see any historical monuments recognizing it as the place where a machine first made what was then called "artificial snow." It happened in the late 1940s and early 1950s, when Mohawk founder Walt Schoenknecht (pronounced "shawn-connect") worked with three buddies to secure the first U.S. patent for the device.

While Mohawk is a small ski area with twenty-six trails, eight lifts and a 650-foot vertical drop, it does attract about 100,000 people per year. Most skiers are from Connecticut, while others take the eighty-mile drive from New York City. And it's not usual to see a few celebrities there. No, I'm not going to name them.

What's also unusual about Mohawk is the fact that it's still run by the same families from the day it first opened. Carol Lugar, daughter of founders Walt and Peg Schoenknecht, is the co-owner and president of Mohawk. Edna Hedden worked as lodge manager from 1947 until her death at age ninety-one. Today, her son, Steve Hedden, is Mohawk's former vice-president. And there are several other Hedden family members working at the ski area.

From the beginning, Mohawk has been dealing with snow-stingy, warm and rainy winters. More than seventy-five years after the first snowmaking system was installed, Mohawk has nearly 100 percent snowmaking coverage. It continues to fight global warming by having a snowmaking system that automatically turns on when temperatures and humidity are good for making snow.

The snow gods were smiling when the Mohawk Mountain ski area opened in December 1947—a blizzard dumped nearly two feet of snow. The following winters, however, had little natural snow. It got so bad that Walt Schoenknecht had 750 tons of ice blocks trucked to Mohawk. There, over a two-day period, ice was crushed and spread onto ski trails. Crushed ice had been used before at ski jumping competitions, but never at a ski area. The crushed ice on the slopes sold lots of lift tickets and garnered free publicity from most northeastern newspapers, including the *New York Daily News*.

Then there was the time Schoenknecht spread pine needles and hay on a grassy trail to allow people to ski in October. The trail was especially fast after the bottoms of skis were painted with a mixture of kerosene and paraffin wax.

Walt Schoenknecht's place in ski history would come after he worked with three Connecticut aviation engineers to develop the first snowmaking machine at a ski area and, later, open Vermont's Mount Snow.

After Walt opened Mount Snow in 1954, he was featured in such national magazines as *LIFE* and *Sports Illustrated*, which called him "The Scamp of the Slope" and "Vermont's Phenomenal Snowman." And with Mount Snow's unusual attractions—like a heated outdoor swimming pool, indoor skating rink, Japanese pool gardens and futuristic air cars—some called him the "Walt Disney of Vermont."

Yet Walt's Mount Snow attractions went much further than the off-slope attractions that skiing purists abhorred. He made trails for all types of skiers, especially for beginners and intermediates. Trails were wider and more enjoyable. He designed the first high-capacity ski lifts and skis-on gondolas.

Walt ran Mount Snow for more than twenty years, before it was purchased by the Sherburne Corporation in 1977. Rising expenses, high interest rates, increasing debt, lousy snow years and the 1973 gas shortage contributed to Schoenknecht losing the Vermont area. He returned home to Mohawk, where he worked until he died of cancer at age sixty-eight.

Spending time at Mohawk is a step back in history. There's the old Pine Lodge, built in 1946, and the classic alpine ski lodge constructed in 1964. Inside that lodge are antique skis, including the rare aluminum skis that were manufactured by the guys who made the snowmaking machine.

On the ski trails, you can still see the old paths where rope tows took skiers to the summit. There's also a small stone tower, built by CCC crews nearly one hundred years ago. You can also ski the first downhill ski trail, which was carved in 1939. Even in winter, you can drive your vehicle to the top of Mohawk Mountain and see the peaks of the Catskills, Taconic and Berkshire Mountains.

Another of the ski area's attractions is its short drive for millions of people to enjoy all that Mohawk and its history have to offer.

THE MOUNTAIN, THE LAND
AND THE PEOPLE

Mohawk Mountain in Cornwall may not be the highest hill in Connecticut, but it's steeped in history.

It was here that Native Americans are said to have lit signal fires from the 1,683-foot summit to warn of the invading Mohawk tribe from the west.

Charcoal made from northwest Connecticut forests fired blast furnaces to smelt locally mined iron ore to make cannons in the American Revolution. One of those iron furnaces was started by Ethan Allen, a Connecticut native who led Vermont's Green Mountain Boys in the pivotal capture of Fort Ticonderoga, New York.

In the Great Depression in the 1930s, young men in the Civilian Conservation Corps blazed Mohawk's first ski trails, built miles of roads, erected fire towers and planted millions of trees.

It was here that a wealthy New York City brother and sister purchased thousands of acres and later donated them to Connecticut for state parks and forests.

And in the mid-twentieth century, there was Connecticut native Walt Schoenknecht, a tall, lanky former marine and avid skier who leased one hundred acres in the Mohawk State Forest to create Connecticut's largest ski area in 1947.

After a successful first season, Schoenknecht's ski area faced a winter with little snow. He dreamed of other ways to cover ski trails when there was no natural snow. In some regards, Schoenknecht was one of the first to confront the effects of global warming. His first attempt to provide a slippery slope for skiers was spreading 750 tons of crushed ice on a trail.

The view from the summit of Mohawk Mountain shows Connecticut's highest peaks, including Bear Mountain to the right. *Author's collection.*

Three of Schoenknecht's buddies who were aviation engineers were also in the same dilemma. Art Hunt, Wayne Pierce and Dave Richey manufactured skis. And in the snowless winter, few people were buying their skis. Working with Schoenknecht, the engineers created the first machine to make snow at a ski area. This first snowmaking system was installed at Mohawk Mountain in 1950. Within a decade, snowmaking would revolutionize—and help save—ski areas from crippling, snow-stingy winters.

Over the years, the work of Schoenknecht—and the Milford, Connecticut engineers who helped achieve this snowmaking dream—has been a footnote in history. Decades ago, there were newspaper and magazine articles in *LIFE* and *Sports Illustrated* that nicknamed Schoenknecht the "Phenomenal Snowman." *LIFE* magazine called him "The Scamp of the Slope." Today, he and the engineers are mostly forgotten.

There's also scant mention of a New Haven, Connecticut ski club that was the nexus that brought together people whose ambitious Yankee ingenuity forever changed skiing. At a club meeting at the New Haven YMCA, Schoenknecht met his future wife, Peg Moss. Together, they would create Connecticut's oldest and largest ski area.

One of Mohawk Mountain's first ski patrollers—Preston Smith of Guilford—later opened the Killington ski area in central Vermont. He shared Schoenknecht's drive and vision to create the Northeast's largest ski resort. Smith's Killington-based Sherburne Company later purchased Walt Schoenknecht's Mount Snow ski resort in 1977.

Mohawk has survived years of poor winters, tornados, a pandemic and a changing world.

Mohawk
Mountain
founder Walt
Schoenknecht.
*Mohawk Mountain
ski area.*

TALLEST TREES, HIGHEST PEAKS AND FEWER PEOPLE

Located in the Litchfield County towns of Cornwall and Goshen, the 3,300-acre Mohawk Mountain State Forest has panoramic views of the Catskill, Taconic and Berkshire Mountains.

This rugged area of Connecticut is known by several names: the Northwest Hills, the Litchfield Hills, the southern Berkshires and the Northwest Highlands. Most just call it Litchfield County, which includes twenty-one towns. The terrain varies from gently rolling hills in the south and east to more mountainous land in the northwest. The county's longest river, the Housatonic, carved a deep valley that runs 149 miles from the Massachusetts Berkshires to Long Island Sound.

Connecticut's northwest corner has the most forestland (81 percent), highest elevation (2,380 feet) and the smallest population. It also has the

Gold's Pines Natural Area Preserve in Cornwall, Connecticut, has the tallest tree in the state, an eastern white pine, standing at 155 feet. *Author's collection.*

tallest tree in the state: an eastern white pine standing at 155 feet, in Gold's Pines Natural Area Preserve. The entrance to the preserve is on the south side of Route 128, one mile from the covered bridge in West Cornwall. If you've seen redwood trees on the Pacific coast, you'll likely be disappointed with Connecticut's tree giants. While tall, the pines are spindly and the trunks small. The lack of markers makes finding the tallest tree in the state difficult.

Cathedral Pines in Cornwall was once New England's largest stand of old-growth white pine and hemlock trees. But that ended on July 10, 1989, when three tornados devastated the area. A trail still traverses the intact portion of the tract where Connecticut's third-tallest white pine stands at 151 feet. Cathedral Pines is located off Essex Hill Road. When he was twelve, Walt Schoenknecht hiked through Cathedral Pines; it was his first visit to Cornwall, Connecticut.

Today, Cornwall—home of the Mohawk Mountain ski area—has the most forestland in Connecticut. Much of the land is state forest and wildlife sanctuaries, earning Cornwall the title of "Greenest Town in Connecticut."

The Cathedral Pines were a popular tourist attraction from the late nineteenth century to July 10, 1989, when tornados blew down most of the two-hundred-year-old trees. *Cornwall Historical Society.*

Litchfield is the only county in the state that has lost population. It's a place where deaths exceed the number of births. With a population of just 1,567, Cornwall has a population density of just 31 people per square mile, according to the U.S. Census Bureau.

The area seems far removed from the I-95 and 91 expressways and the urban/suburban sprawl of shopping centers, subdivisions and electronic billboards in central and southern Connecticut. Apart from the "bigger" towns like Torrington, New Milford and Winsted, most towns in Litchfield County have few, if any, traffic lights. The only time there is traffic gridlock on local roads is during peak fall foliage season.

Even the climate seems different—and cooler—in this rural corner of Connecticut. Litchfield County's high elevation and microclimates give it the biggest snowfall and coldest temperatures in the state. The county's lowest temperature—minus thirty-two degrees—was recorded in Falls Village on February 16, 1943, according to the National Weather Service.

WEST CORNWALL'S ICONIC COVERED BRIDGE

There is a deep sense of history in the Northwest Hills. Driving on the area's two-lane roads, it's hard to miss the Colonial houses, covered bridges, white steepled churches, historic villages and ancient cemeteries. With its iconic covered bridge over the Housatonic River, village greens and panoramic views from Mohawk's summit, Cornwall seems more like Vermont than Connecticut.

The red covered bridge in West Cornwall is a vestige of earlier times. The present bridge between Cornwall and Sharon, Connecticut—estimated to have been built in 1864—was not the first to cross the Housatonic. There have been bridges at its location since at least 1762, rebuilt time and time again. Floodwaters, washouts, ice floes, hurricanes, rotting wood and inadequate maintenance are among the causes of bridge problems. One of the more unusual incidents happened in 1945, when a twenty-ton oil truck fell through the bridge's wooden floor.

There were attempts to abandon the covered bridge and build a new concrete and steel span that would have overflown the village of West Cornwall. In 1961, the Connecticut General Assembly passed an act that would preserve the covered bridge if a new bridge was built.

Connecticut's most iconic covered bridge, in West Cornwall, is estimated to have been built in 1864. Earlier bridges were destroyed by floods and spring ice floes. *Author's collection.*

Then, in 1969, after the state decided to replace the bridge, a campaign was mounted to convince people that the covered bridge could and should be repaired without replacement. The preservationists won; the structure was jacked up two feet, and its abutments and pier were raised for better protection against high water. Its roadway was replaced with a new independently suspended steel deck topped with wooden flooring.

In 1973, the Federal Highway Administration called the bridge work one of the nation's "Outstanding Example of the Preservation, Restoration or Relocations of Historic Sites." In 1975, the bridge was added to the U.S. Interior Department's National Register of Historic Places.

Connecticut has only three historic covered bridges. Apart from West Cornwall, there is the two-lane Bulls Bridge in Gaylordsville, built in 1841, and the pedestrian-only Comstock Bridge in East Hampton, built in 1873. In the mid- to late 1800s, there were many covered bridges in Connecticut that were heavily concentrated in western Connecticut over the Housatonic, Naugatuck and Farmington Rivers.

GEOLOGICAL CHANGES TRANSFORM CONNECTICUT

Blame the glaciers and millions of years of erosion for Connecticut's mini mountains. About 480 million years ago, these mountains were as high as the Alps and the Rocky Mountains.

At 2,316 feet, Bear Mountain in Salisbury is the highest peak that lies solely in Connecticut. In the 1940s, the U.S. Geological Survey determined that the highest point in the state—2,380 feet—was on the south slope of Mount Frissell on the Connecticut/Massachusetts border. The bedrock in the Northwest Hills and mountains, part of the Appalachian Mountain range, are more than 1 billion years old.

Today, it's almost impossible to imagine how Connecticut was eons ago. Volcanic activity millions of years ago helped shape the life and landscape of Connecticut. East and West Rock in New Haven and Sleeping Giant in Hamden were created by three major lava flows.

And what about dinosaurs and monstrous mammoths? They lived in this land that would be named Connecticut. The name comes from a Native American name—*quinatucquet*—roughly meaning "beside the long tidal river."

In the central part of Connecticut, thousands of dinosaur tracks were unearthed during a highway construction project in 1966. Among them were tracks from Dilophosaurus, the first large carnivorous dinosaur in the early Jurassic period. There was even the "Farmington Mastodon," unearthed in 1913. The mastodon's skeleton is the most complete one found in New England, dating back about fifteen thousand years ago, according to Yale's Peabody Museum.

During the last ice age, about twenty-one thousand years ago, much of Connecticut was covered by a massive glacier at least one mile thick. As the glacier moved south from Canada, it picked up boulders and sediment from the earth's surface.

The ice sheet eroded mountains, formed lakes and scattered glacial tills of silt, sand, gravel and boulders. As the glacier melted about eighteen thousand years ago, great rivers of water flowed downhill, carving deep valleys in the hills. Large quantities of clay and sand were carried down to the shoreline, creating the coastal lowland on Long Island Sound.

Connecticut has three major geologic regions: the western and eastern highlands' older metamorphic rock and the central valley composed of basalt and sandstone.

Today, the effects of the glaciers can be seen across Connecticut. Many of the state's stone walls were built by the early settlers with rocks left by the

This is an oil on canvas painting of Bear Mountain in Salisbury, Connecticut, by John Bunyan Bristol, created in 1885–86. *Connecticut Museum of Culture and History.*

On the summit of Mohawk Mountain, scratches and gouges cut into the bedrock show where the glacier moved about twenty-one thousand years ago. *Author's collection.*

On August 13, 1913, the skeletal remains of the largest mastodon in New England were found in Farmington, Connecticut, on Alfred Pope's country home, Hill-Stead. *Connecticut State Library.*

melting glaciers. The larger boulders and rocks in forestland and fields are called "glacial erratics."

On the summit of Mohawk Mountain, near the site of the old lookout tower, are scratches and gouges cut into the bedrock that show where the glacier moved.

Mohawk Mountain's Black Spruce Bog was likely formed as a "sink hole" after Connecticut's last glacial period about 15,500 years ago. A large block of glacial ice left a depression about forty feet deep that filled with water. Gradually, plants filled from the edges toward the center. The unique natural area is considered an outstanding example of a late-stage peat bog. The best time to visit is in winter.

After the ice sheet melted, the land lay bare of vegetation. Scientists believe that vegetation returned from seeds that were either buried in ice, brought by birds or blown from warmer neighboring areas.

Except for a few farm fields, the northern view from the summit of Mohawk Mountain is heavily forested with northern hardwoods and pine. Looking to the south, the terrain is mostly hills and river valleys. The eastern and western views are blocked by tall trees.

More than sixty miles away, on the southern horizon, a white plume can be seen rising on clear, chilly days—not a signal fire to warn of invading Mohawks, but rather a gas-fired power plant in Bridgeport, Connecticut.

THE FIRST PEOPLE

In his 1851 book *Indians of Connecticut*, historian John William DeForest estimated that there were no more than between six and seven thousand Native Americans living in the state between 1630 and 1635. The tribes were part of the Algonquin people, one of the most populous and widespread North American cultural and language groups.

Most tribes, DeForest wrote, "were clustered in small groups along the shore of Long Island Sound and along the larger rivers, where the lands were best adapted for corn and where they could depend largely on fishing for their food supply."

Tribes included the Quinnipiacs on the western shoreline and the Pequots and Mohegan in southeastern Connecticut. The Paugussett and the Potatuck tribes ranged from Milford to Fairfield to the hills of Newtown, Roxbury and Woodbury. There were Agawams in north-central Connecticut and the Nipmucks in the northeast.

"The occasional raids of the Mohawks from the Hudson River," DeForest wrote, "were a further discouragement to the Connecticut tribes from inhabiting the western forests of the state." The fear of the Mohawk tribe led to the naming of Mohawk Mountain. While there is no direct historical evidence of the signal fires, the words *legend*, *tradition* and *custom* often appear in writings on how Mohawk Mountain got its name.

A June 30, 1882 article in the *New Hartford (CT) Tribune* noted:

*The Indians of Western Connecticut suffered exceedingly from incursions
of the fierce Mohawks from central New York, who made an annual
incursion through this section on their way to the fishing grounds of Bantam
and Milford and the wampum [clam] beds of Branford.*

*And, in order to protect themselves from these incursions, they established
a system of watchfire stations to warn the Indians of Connecticut of the
approach of their ancient foe, the Mohawks. Mohawk Mountain was chosen
as the central signal mountain, from whence the name Mohawk Mountain.
The place was well chosen, for a watch fire on the mountain could be seen
from the top of every hill between the Hudson and Connecticut Rivers.*

A 1940 report by the State Forest Commission stated, "Tradition has
it that Mohawk Mountain derives its name from the custom of the local
Indians of burning signal fires on the summit to warn their kinsmen to the
south of the approach of the dreaded Mohawks from the north and west."

According to Harriet Lydia Clark's *History of East Cornwall*, although the
Mohawks did not live in northwest Connecticut, a "legend" said that local
tribes lit signal fires on the summit of the mountain to warn tribes to the
south that Mohawks were approaching.

An illustration of a Native American family that appeared in John William DeForest's 1851
book *Indians of Connecticut*. No credit was given to the artist.

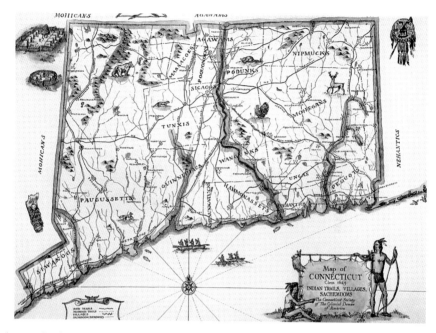

A reproduction of a circa 1625 map shows Indian villages, tribes and trails It was created in 1930 for the Connecticut Society of the Colonial Dames of America by Mathias Speiss.

DeForest wrote that the Mohawks' "very appearance excited consternation; a cry of alarm would extend from hill to hill, and the natives would fly for safety to swamps and thickets, or to their fortresses. A large part of the inhabitants of the country west of the Connecticut [river] became their subjects; and every year, two old Mohawks might be seen going from village to village to collect tribute, and haughtily issuing orders from the great council at Onondaga."

As more white settlers arrived in Connecticut, "the Indians were pushed back into the western wilderness, so that probably their numbers in Litchfield County increased very much in Litchfield County between 1630 and 1720; but their total numbers across the whole state decreased proportionately much more," DeForest wrote.

The locations of present-day Route 7 and Route 44 roughly follow the paths of old Indian trails, named by colonial historians as the Berkshire and the Northwest paths.

The Indigenous tribes also faced another deadly threat in the 1630s: European diseases transmitted by traders and settlers. The tribes were vulnerable to the plague, smallpox, cholera, tuberculosis and childhood diseases like measles and chickenpox.

The epidemic of diseases started in eastern Massachusetts around 1616–19. Around Windsor, Connecticut, in 1633, a plague killed many of the local tribe members. Dutch traders estimated that more than 90 percent of the tribe's members died, according to the Yale University Press book *Connecticut's Indigenous Peoples*. It was followed a year later by an outbreak of smallpox. The epidemic later spread to the Quinnipiac tribe on the shoreline.

Smallpox also broke out in the westernmost Indian village near present-day New Milford. It is believed that smallpox was brought by men from New Haven who established a trading post there in 1646.

And then there were wars. On May 26, 1637, the Pequot tribe in southeastern Connecticut lost more than four hundred men, women and children when their fort was attacked and burned to the ground by the English and their Native allies. In 1675–76, King Philip's War between the English colonies and the Native tribes further reduced the number of New England Indians.

Many of the survivors moved out of New England. Others—like the remnants of the Paugussetts, Potatucks and Tunxis tribes—settled on the four-hundred-acre Schaghticoke reservation in Kent, Connecticut.

Today, Connecticut has several Indigenous Indian tribes recognized by the state: the Schaghticokes, Paucatucks, Eastern Pequots, Mashantucket Pequots, Mohegans and the Golden Hill Paugussetts. Only two, the Mashantucket Pequot and Mohegan tribes, have received federal recognition, allowing the tribes to operate casinos on their sovereign nation lands.

THE FIRST SETTLERS

When the first colonies of Connecticut were founded in the early 1600s, the northwest area of the state was known as a "howling wilderness" and the "terrible Greenwoods." The unbroken forest had a few narrow Indian trails that were barely wide enough for a horse. There were blackflies, mosquitoes, rattlesnakes and soil filled with rocks and boulders.

The first outpost by Europeans in the state was established in 1633, a Dutch fort on the bank of the Connecticut River—the future site of Hartford. Two years later, the English established their own fort at the end of the Connecticut River in Saybrook. And in 1638, the New Haven Colony was established along the Connecticut shoreline. All of these settlements were either on the shoreline or in the fertile soil in river valleys. It would take another century before the first towns in northwest Connecticut were settled.

In 1686, the Connecticut General Court adopted a plan designed to prevent the king of England and his agent in America, Governor Edmund Andros of the newly constituted Dominion of New England, from taking those lands away from Connecticut control. As a stopgap measure, colonial authorities deeded the entire undeveloped northwest Connecticut land to the towns of Hartford and Windsor.

With Connecticut's population growing, the General Court decided to survey the land in the northwest hills in 1731–32. A Historic and Architectural Resource Survey of Cornwall report in 2000 described how settlers came into possession of the lands:

> *The rapid settlement push into the Northwest Highlands in the first half of the eighteenth century consisted of two separate but related developments: creation of seven daughter towns of Hartford and Windsor, and auction of seven additional towns in the watershed of the Housatonic River to residents of the entire colony.*
>
> *Rather than give the land to any town or group, colonial authorities determined to auction shares in seven proposed new townships to the highest bidders, with sales to be conducted at several dispersed sites across Connecticut. To validate their deeds, successful bidders (or their agents) were required to build a house 18 feet square and seven feet from sill to plate, clear and fence six acres, and dwell there three years. A further stipulation reserved 300 acres in each new town for support of Yale College.*

Settlement of Connecticut's Northwest Hills by English immigrants largely displaced the remaining Native Americans. As early as 1720, several Dutch families moved east from the Hudson River Valley and acquired land near present-day Salisbury. Twenty years later, Cornwall formally became an incorporated town.

The first settlers encountered many challenges in the rugged, heavily forested land. "Simply clearing the land proved daunting, with endless acres of trees to be felled and uncounted tons of stones removed from fields. Wild animals proved an ever-present danger, and most towns offered bounties on bears, wolves, mountain lions, and rattlesnakes," the survey report noted.

A 1938 Works Progress Administration guidebook also noted that "many settlers died during the early days of Cornwall's first settlement (1738–40) when cattle were kept alive only by giving them venison broth, and when children froze in their beds. This was not a kindly country…only the very poor or the very brave settled here."

THE "ARSENAL OF THE REVOLUTION"

In 1731, surveyors Ezekiel Ashley and John Pell made an unexpected discovery: iron ore on "Ore Hill" in Salisbury, Connecticut. Four years after the discovery, the first iron furnace was in operation in Lime Rock. Before the Revolutionary War, the furnace produced iron goods such as tools and stoves for settlers.

The ore was from iron-rich sediments that formed more than 450 million years ago after two continental collisions created the Appalachian Mountains.

Ethan Allen, a Patriot and war hero, was born in Litchfield, Connecticut, on January 21, 1738. When Ethan was a boy, his family moved to Cornwall to start a farm after new townships were formed in the Northwest Hills.

While Allen is best known for the capture of Fort Ticonderoga, New York, in the early days of the Revolution, he was also one of the founders of the Salisbury iron furnace, which produced more than eight hundred cannons for colonial troops.

In December 1776, Connecticut governor Jonathan Trumbull's Committee of Safety seized the Salisbury furnace to ensure that General George Washington's army would have a steady supply of cannons. "It is of the greatest importance for the safety and defence [*sic*] of this and the United States of America, that the foundry of cannon should be continued in Salisbury," the resolution said, according to General Assembly records. Seizing the foundry would produce "a large number [of cannons] to be sent to the northern forts and for the ships, and they are also greatly needed for our immediate defence [*sic*]."

Plans were made so that if the furnace and foundry were destroyed by the British, it would quickly be repaired. Armed guards surrounded the Salisbury furnace, which operated around the clock, seven days a week. With its production of cannons and other armaments, the Salisbury furnace became known as one of the "Arsenals of the Revolution."

During the American Revolution, other towns in northwest Connecticut played important roles in supplying food, supplies and munitions for soldiers to the Patriot army. Near the summit of Mohawk Mountain, there was

One of the best-preserved iron ore blast furnaces can be seen off Route 44 in Canaan, Connecticut. The towering nineteenth-century Beckley Furnace is on the Blackberry River. *Connecticut Historical Society.*

also a small shop that made flintlock rifles for Revolutionary War soldiers, according to Cornwall Historical Society records.

The town of Litchfield, founded in 1719, had two military depots on a key turnpike connecting Boston and West Point. In July 1776, the lead statue of English King George III was torn down from its pedestal on Bowling Green in New York City. Pieces of the king's statue were taken to Litchfield, where townspeople cast more than forty-two thousand bullets from this material.

During the 1800s, there were about forty blast furnaces in the upper Housatonic River region in places like West Cornwall, Sharon, Lime Rock and on Mount Riga in Salisbury. One of the best-preserved iron ore blast furnaces can be seen off Route 44 in Canaan.

The decline of the iron industry began after the Civil War, when railroads provided easy access to iron ore and coal in Pennsylvania. The iron age ended in northwest Connecticut when it became cheaper to smelt the more plentiful low-grade ores from western states.

THE BEGINNING OF THE
MOHAWK MOUNTAIN SKI AREA

The next time you visit Kent Falls, Macedonia or Mohawk Mountain State Parks, pause and give thanks to Alain and Margaret "May" White. If it weren't for these two very generous people, northwest Connecticut would look much different than it does today. Between 1908 and 1912, the Whites bought and preserved forever more than nine thousand acres as a memorial to their parents, John Jay and Louise White.

A total of 5,745 acres was acquired by Connecticut as gifts and funds from the White Memorial Foundation. Much of the land donated to Connecticut formed the nucleus of its most rural state parks and forests. The land donations included 2,100 acres at Mohawk Mountain State Park and Mohawk Mountain State Forest in Cornwall and Goshen; 2,000 acres at Macedonia Brook in Kent; 200 acres at Kent Falls; and 400 acres at Peoples State Forest in Barkhamsted.

Today, property held by the White Memorial Foundation totals about 4,000 acres of forests, fields and wetlands throughout Litchfield County and near Bantam Lake in Litchfield and Morris, Connecticut. With 9,461 surface acres, Bantam is the state's largest naturally formed freshwater lake. Because the foundation properties are wildlife sanctuaries, there is no hunting and trapping. The foundation is the largest wildlife refuge and nature center in Connecticut.

The land's diversity of habitats makes it one of the best birding sites in the state, according to Audubon Connecticut. Since 1958, 246 species of birds have been recorded on the foundation's lands. The thirty-five miles of

Alain and Margaret White are shown with their father, John Jay White. The White children donated more than 5,700 acres to Connecticut in memory of their parents. *White Memorial Foundation.*

woodland roads, hiking trails and boardwalks offer plenty of birdwatching opportunities. And with an average snowfall of fifty inches, the generally flat trails are ideal for cross-country skiing and snowshoeing.

Alain and May were the children of a New York City lawyer and real estate tycoon who built a summer estate, named Whitehall, in Litchfield, Connecticut. The Whites purchased the land decades after the peak of the iron industry. Much of the property was abandoned farmland or heavily deforested. When the Whites bought the property in the early twentieth century, prices for real estate were just a few dollars per acre.

By the 1870s, more than 70 percent of the region's trees had been cut down to make charcoal for the iron blast furnaces. Annually, it took about six hundred acres of trees to make charcoal for each furnace.

After purchasing the land, the Whites had thousands of trees planted. The Whites' land purchases and the arrival of Civilian Conservation Corps crews in the 1930s Great Depression helped save and restore the remaining forests and land. Another job for the CCC crews was cutting ski trails—the beginning of what would become Connecticut's largest ski area.

A 1938 tour book, published by the Works Progress Administration, described the people of Litchfield County: "The natives are shy and reticent, but the summer folk and weekenders add considerable life and gaiety to the region until winter snows blanket the countryside." It also noted, "Winter sports enjoy limited popularity but are growing in importance."

THE FIRST TOURISTS OF LITCHFIELD COUNTY

Many of the first Litchfield County tourists came via the Housatonic Railroad to New Preston, Kent, Kent Falls, Cornwall Bridge and West Cornwall, where the iconic covered bridge still stands. The railroads and country inns advertised excursions into Litchfield County with places to stay overnight. A popular tourist attraction was the Cathedral Pines, a large grove of old-growth trees.

The Housatonic Railroad was chartered in 1836 connecting Bridgeport and Canaan. Service continued with a connection in Stockbridge with the Western Railroad of Massachusetts. In New Milford, the line tracked over the Housatonic, traveling along the east side of the river on an old Indian trail. In 1872, the Shepaug Valley Railroad ran between Bethel and Litchfield. The line was operated until being abandoned in 1948. Service continued to decline when roads improved and automobiles became more affordable. The last passenger service on the original Housatonic Railroad was on April 30, 1971. The current owner of the railroad hopes to restore passenger service.

As they do today, early tourists were drawn by the scenic vistas from the summit of Mohawk Mountain, hiking trails, cascading waterfalls, lakes and streams.

In the late nineteenth century, residents formed the Mohawk Tower Corporation to raise money to purchase land on the summit and build a carriage road and observation tower. A condition of the land purchase stated that "it shall revert to the Hunts Lyman Iron Company if there is any wine, cider, ale, beer or any intoxicating liquors ever sold on said land."

To this day, the Mohawk Mountain ski area's lease with the state bans the sale of alcohol. It is the only ski area in Connecticut that doesn't have a bar.

The first wooden observation tower on the Mohawk Mountain summit opened on July 4, 1883. One newspaper report said that two thousand people attended. A cabin was built near the tower to sell food to guests or provide overnight accommodations. In 1898, the wooden tower was blown down in a windstorm.

In the 1880s, the summit of Mohawk Mountain became a popular tourist destination. A wood cabin offered food and overnight accommodations. *Cornwall Historical Society.*

Today, distant northern views of the Taconic, Catskill and Berkshire Mountains remain impressive. Rolling hills and valleys are seen in the south. Vistas in the east and west are mostly obscured by tall trees.

The most unattractive sights on the summit are two communication towers not accessible to the public. A former forest fire watchtower is surrounded by round antenna dishes and barbed wire. In 1953, the state made an agreement with AT&T to place a booster microwave repeater station at the summit. The 65-foot tower has changed ownership over the years and has been modified. In 1979, a 180-foot tower and equipment building were erected to improve communication between public safety organizations. The tower was built to eliminate dead spots in communications caused by the hilly terrain.

Since 1988, there has been an air quality monitoring station on Mohawk's summit. It is one of fourteen stations across Connecticut that track air quality and measure pollutants like particulate matter, ozone and carbon monoxide. According to the American Lung Association, Litchfield County is rated B for the fewest high ozone days, averaging one per year; Fairfield County is highest, with thirty-eight days when ozone alerts are issued.

The only remains of the last public observation tower, erected in 1974 and removed in 2008, are concrete supports dug into glacial rock.

Today, most people going to the summit travel by motor vehicles. There's a small parking lot and a place to turn around for the return trip. Toumey Road, from Route 4 to the summit, is kept open year-round to provide access to the communication towers. While it's kept plowed in winter, the road is narrow near the summit and can be icy at times. Sometimes, winds are so strong that it's difficult to open vehicle doors.

Most of Mohawk Mountain remained private property until it was donated to the state by Alain and May White in 1922. At one time there were several houses on the flat land below Mohawk's summit.

In 1914, Seymour Cunningham of Litchfield bought an abandoned farm and gradually built up a large estate. Part of the then meadows were used as grazing grounds for Cunningham's sheep. In what was the first forestry work on Mohawk Mountain, he also planted seventy-five acres of pine trees.

Cunningham also built a thirty-foot circular stone observation tower that still stands. It no longer has a roof or stairway. Vandals have also spray-painted the lower sections of the tower and damaged its stone fireplace. The tower, once named "Aerie," was designed like an old Irish watchtower. According to the *Irish Times*, Ireland's Napoleonic-era coastal watchtowers

Today, the most unattractive sights on the summit are two communication towers. A former fire watchtower is surrounded by barbed wire. *Author's collection.*

In 1914, Seymour Cunningham bought an abandoned farm and built an estate and stone observation tower, which still stands. *Author's collection.*

were built to warn of an invasion by the French. An invasion was averted by Napoleon's defeat in the 1815 Battle of Waterloo in the Netherlands.

In 1920, Cunningham decided to sell his property to Alain White after his attempt to close a nearby road and block access to Mohawk's summit was rejected by Cornwall officials. White later gave Cunningham's property to the state and an area around Mohawk Pond to the YMCA, where he was a director.

The state formally took possession of 867 acres during a meeting of the State Park and Forest Commission on July 19, 1921. The meeting was held inside Cunningham's stone tower.

Traveling on roads in the 1920s and early 1930s was very difficult. Before the state took ownership of Mohawk Mountain, "the highway from Torrington to Goshen and Cornwall was of the old-type dirt road. This was also true of the road from Goshen to Litchfield," according to a 1940 state report.

The first state highway, now Route 7, was built north from New Milford and ended at Cornwall Bridge. "All of these old dirt roads were practically impassable during the spring season," the state report asserted. "The grades [steepness] were excessive and in the day of the Model T Ford many a car of that type was seen backing up a hill due to the insufficient gas in the tank to run forward to the carburetor."

Around 1928, the state highway (now Route 4) from Torrington to Goshen was constructed. By 1930, "a good system of hard surfaced roads had been built throughout the area eliminating many of the excessive grades," the state report said.

Today, a stone marker indicating the highway boundary of Route 4 is still visible by the Torrington Country Club in Goshen. Heading west, it is located on the left side of Route 4 less than a half mile from the Torrington and Goshen town line. The marker, between twelve and eighteen inches high, is engraved with the initials "CHD." The initials stand for Connecticut Highway Department, a state agency that became part of the Connecticut Department of Transportation in 1969.

The Goshen marker was installed shortly after the CHD began preparing highway maps in 1926. "The early years of the 1900s were years during which Highway Department and construction contractors learned and moved forward together in the art and science of roadway construction," according to the Connecticut Department of Transportation's history page. "Some of the new methods being tried included drilling and blasting of rock; sub-base, drainage and concrete paving processes; construction machinery development; and the use of small gauge railroads with steam engines to haul materials to the job site."

After World War I, the steam engines were replaced by gasoline engines, according to DOT's history page. "In the winter of 1922–23, the first gas-powered shovel was brought to Connecticut, and in the spring of 1923 [it] was first used on federal-aid road construction from Litchfield to Torrington."

CCC ARRIVES AT MOHAWK MOUNTAIN

A Great Depression program that gave millions of unemployed men jobs in parks and forests would lead to the development of the first ski trails in the nation.

The Great Depression began with the 1929 stock market crash and continued to around 1939. Millions of people lost their jobs. It followed the 1920s, when a long boom in stock prices reached record levels. By the end of 1932, they had reached rock bottom.

Franklin D. Roosevelt's election as president in 1932 would bring a "New Deal" for Americans. In March 1933, FDR called Congress to an emergency session to pass the Emergency Conservation Act, which included the Civilian Conservation Corps (CCC).

The immediate goal of the CCC was to put millions of unemployed men back to work. The environmental and conservation work included planting millions of trees, building roads and constructing lodges, as well as forest fire protection.

Connecticut had twenty-one CCC camps from 1933 and 1942. The volunteers for these camps were unemployed young men between eighteen and twenty-five years old and, later, World War I veterans. They were paid thirty dollars per month, twenty-five of which were sent directly to their families.

In Litchfield County, CCC camps were set up at Mohawk Mountain in Cornwall, Housatonic Meadows in Sharon, Black Rock in Thomaston and Macedonia in Kent. Each camp had 250 men. Mohawk Mountain's Camp Toumey (named after James W. Toumey, dean of the Yale Forestry School) operated from June 25, 1933, to July 26, 1941.

Camp Toumey CCC crews built a road from Route 4, through the forest and to the summit; planted trees and removed dead and diseased ones; brushed out sixty miles of wood roads and created nineteen water ponds to

Connecticut had twenty-one CCC camps from 1933 and 1942, including one at Mohawk Mountain. Among the jobs for CCC crews was fighting forest fires. *Cornwall Historical Society.*

fight fires; blazed a thirty-mile trail system for hikers; and created the first picnic grounds with fireplaces, tables, privies and shelters. Some of those large stone fireplaces are still standing. You can see the fireplaces by taking Allyn Road off Route 4 near the Mohawk Bison Farm (yes, they raise bison). Past the bison farm, the road becomes steep. Look to the left as you drive up Mohawk Mountain—there's two fireplaces before you reach the park headquarters. One appears to have been part of a large building, and the other is a standalone fireplace that may have been a place to cook outdoor meals.

The first ski trails at Mohawk date back to the 1936–37 season, when CCC crews turned forest roads into two cross-country ski trails. A 1937 pamphlet by the Connecticut Forest and Park Association provided details of the trails:

> *Mohawk Mountain on Route Four (Torrington to Cornwall Bridge) and Toumey Road, which leads south through the Mohawk State Forest from the top of Bunker Hill, two miles west of West Goshen.*
>
> *Trail No. One—west side of Toumey Road, following old road to Route 4; length one-half mile, width, 12 feet, maximum grade 13 degrees, exposure northwest.*

Trail No. Two—starts at the Lookout Tower, east down [the] ridge and then by alternate routes to Toumey Road; length 1.3 miles, width 12 feet, vertical descent 200 feet, maximum grade 20 degrees, exposure north and east.

Current maps of Mohawk Mountain show cross-country ski trails just in the northern sections of the Mohawk State Forest. The Nordic ski trails are located off Toumey Road past the Mohawk Mountain ski area's summit on the wooded paths of the Tracy and Baldwin Roads.

Other ski trails are in the southern section of the Mohawk State Forest on early dirt roads named Johnson, Rock Box and the Tornado Roads (the longest at 1.3 miles). Snowmobile and general use trails in the southern section of the Mohawk State Forest include Bear Swamp, Hubbell, Wadhams and Hancock Roads.

The first downhill ski trail was built for the 1939–40 season. It was designed by Rolf Holdvedt under the direction of the Connecticut Winter Sports Association and the State Forest Department. This trail—named Mohawk—is the oldest alpine ski run at Mohawk. The trail, about a mile long and thirty-five to fifty feet wide, starts at Pinnacle area on the northwest side of Mohawk Mountain. Lack of snow delayed the opening of this trail until January 1940. This was a "hike-up" ski trail because no rope tows existed at the time.

"The trail was 7/10 of a mile long, had several sharp turns and a very deep drop," reported the Camp Toumey newspaper, *Mohawk Overlook*. "At the end of the trail was a substantial shelter for 20 or more people and fireplaces were located nearby for warming one's food. From the beginning, this ski run had been very popular and at the end of the season a Connecticut State Ski Meet was held here and the drop from the top to the bottom was made in 48 seconds."

A small stone tower built by the CCC still stands at the top of the trail. It's hard to miss on the right at the terminus of the Mohawk chairlift.

Besides Mohawk, CCC workers and ski club members carved ski trails at other camps in Connecticut:

- At Camp Stuart along the Salmon River in East Hampton, the Appalachian Ski Club laid out three trails: novice, intermediate and expert. The 1,400-foot-long expert trail was considered one of the toughest in the state, with its thirty-degree maximum grade.

- At Camp Robinson at the Tunxis State Forest in East Hartland, there were several ski trails and open slopes on abandoned farmland. CCC crews also built a large parking lot and a log cabin for skiers. The 1937 ski pamphlet said the expert ski trail was a half-mile long, had a 632-foot vertical drop and a 37 percent maximum grade. There was also a seven-mile cross-country trail in the Tunxis forest.

In his book *Connecticut Civilian Conservation Camps: History, Memories & Legacy of the CCC,* author Martin Podskoch wrote that the cabin was heated by a massive stone fireplace to the south of the ski slope. "Today the slope is overgrown and unrecognizable. The dirt road to the cabin is lined by some stone walls and cul-de-sacs that were built by the CCC. No early ski facility survives in the Mohawk State Forest, making the Tunxis Forest Ski Cabin one of the oldest, if not the oldest, structures associated with downhill skiing in the state."

In the 1930s, the CCC built other ski trails on the bigger mountains of northern New England. Seven ski trails were cut on Mount Mansfield in Stowe, Vermont, including Nose Drive, Lord and Perry Merrill. The CCC's Bear's Den and Wilderness trails are at Burke Mountain.

In New Hampshire, you can still ski on CCC-built trails at Cannon Mountain in Franconia Notch. And then there's the 2.3-mile John Sherburne trail, starting in Tuckerman's Ravine below Mount Washington and dropping 2,200 feet to Route 16 in Pinkham Notch.

In Massachusetts, the CCC's Thunderbolt trail drops two thousand feet over 1.5 miles on Mount Greylock, the state's tallest mountain. Shortly after the trail opened in 1935, thousands watched international ski races there. Today, it remains one of best backcountry ski trails in New England. It is maintained by the Thunderbolt Ski Runners.

SKI TRAINS IN CONNECTICUT

With interest in skiing growing, there came a new way to travel to New England ski areas: the ski train.

The first train left Boston's North Station on January 11, 1931. The Boston and Maine Railroad train carried 196 passengers, mainly members of the Appalachian Mountain Club and the Dartmouth Outdoors Club.

In 1935, the New Haven Railroad ran trains to northern New England ski areas. By 1939–40, the trains were carrying more than 18,500 passengers. *Author's collection.*

The train arrived in Warner, New Hampshire, in the Mount Washington Valley, where passengers enjoyed a variety of winter sports, including cross-country skiing, snowshoeing and sledding.

Beginning in January 1935, the New York, New Haven and Hartford Railroad had ski trains running from New York City, through Connecticut and into western Massachusetts. One of those trains stopped in Norfolk, Connecticut, where ski jumping competitions and Nordic ski races were held at Norfolk Hill, across from the Blackberry River Inn on Route 44.

The branch line railroad was part of what was the Hartford and Connecticut Western Railroad, later absorbed into the New Haven Railroad system. The train brought skiers from Danbury and up to Canaan via the Housatonic Line. The distance from East Canaan to Norfolk was about eight miles.

"A combination of factors, the snow trains, the government relief program which provided the CCC labor for the construction of ski trails brought about a recognition of New England as an ideal winter sports playground," according to a December 8, 1935 *Hartford (CT) Courant* article.

By the 1939–40 season, the New York, New Haven and Hartford Railroad was carrying more than 18,500 passengers on its snow trains. Service was extended with weekend trains traveling to ski areas in northern New England.

The overnight "Ski Meister" train ran to Woodstock and Stowe, Vermont, picking up passengers in New York City, Stamford, South Norwalk, Bridgeport, New Haven, Hartford and Springfield, Massachusetts.

The "Eastern Slope Express" traveled to the Franconia region of New Hampshire. Stops were made in Stamford, South Norwalk, Bridgeport and New Haven.

The one-day "Snow Express" went to Great Barrington, Lee and Pittsfield, Massachusetts. Stops were made in Stamford and South Norwalk.

A one-day snow train also ran from Hartford, Connecticut, to Manchester and East Dorset, Vermont. Shuttle service was provided to the Mount Aeolus and Bromley Mountain ski areas. The train left Hartford at 8:00 a.m., arrived in East Dorset at 11:55 a.m. and departed back to Hartford at 4:55 p.m., arriving there at 9:00 p.m. The cost of the round-trip ticket? Just $2.50.

The beginning of World War II caused the suspension of most ski trains. After the war, the New Haven Railroad operated its last ski train on January 27, 1946.

CALLS FOR CONNECTICUT'S OWN LARGE SKI AREA

On January 21, 1942, *Hartford Courant* writer R.D. Britton, in his "Along the Ski Trails" column, wrote that wartime gas rationing and lack of rubber for car tires was affecting how far Connecticut skiers could travel for skiing. "With rubber, or the lack of it, on every skier's mind, more and more Connecticut skiers are going to be skiing in Connecticut this winter."

Britton was pleased that the Connecticut Development Commission published a pamphlet giving the locations of all public and private ski areas in the state. The brochure provided descriptions of the ski hills, trails, vertical drops and directions to get there. It also listed the nineteen ski clubs in Connecticut.

Britton then raised the idea of having the state develop a ski area. Or at least, get the ball—or snowball—rolling: "Among Connecticut skiers there has been some talk, or possibly wishful thinking, about a large skiing area in the state including an Alpine lift, rope tows, practice slopes, and instructors. The idea is to provide skiers with the same type of partially self-supporting recreational area as many cities provide for golfers….Because of the nature of a ski area, it would have to come under state supervision. The initial outlay would probably be from fifty thousand to a hundred thousand."

Britton wrote that the New Hampshire legislature was considering a bill that would appropriate more than $300,000 to develop a large area at Mount Sunapee. "Arguments against a large area in Connecticut are that we do not get a heavy enough snowfall to warrant the expense and that this is no time to talk of such an outlay when every dollar is needed for defense. Arguments for such an area are that localities such as Norfolk or Hartland have as heavy snowfall as many public developments in New York and Massachusetts, and that the exercise which skiing provides is an excellent body builder for the youngsters and much needed relaxation for their parents."

Britten ended the column by writing, "If this question is discussed at any ski club meeting, will the club report to this column the sentiment of its members?"

MOHAWK MOUNTAIN'S FIRST SKI SEASON

It was a shared love of skiing that brought together the two people who created the Mohawk Mountain ski area.

Before World War II, Walter Robert Schoenknecht and Margaret "Peg" Moss met at a meeting of the Quinnipiac Club, now called the New Haven Ski Club.

Peg was attending the Yale School of Nursing when she met Walt at the meeting, held at the local YMCA. The club was formed on January 6, 1941, by Kirste Hille, the wife of a Yale professor, at the request of Schoenknecht and Marjorie Sand, who worked at the Y. The first meeting drew nearly fifty skiers.

According to the New Haven Ski Club's history, in the late 1940s, Schoenknecht shared with fellow members his goal for the future. "Walter's plan was for a ski area in the town of Cornwall to be known as Mohawk Mountain." That dream would become a reality years later when Mohawk opened in December 1947.

The club's first trips were not to mountains or local ski hills, but rather to the nearby golf course. In search of more challenging terrain, Walt and a group of friends from the Grand Avenue Congregational Church Sunday school cut ski trails in the woods behind his parents' house off Laurel Street in East Haven, Connecticut. A love of the outdoors caused Walt to join the Quinnipiac Canoe Club, the Yale Outing Club and the New Haven Hiking Club. One summer, he bicycled across Maine, sleeping in youth hostels and barns.

There would be more challenging ski trips when one of his friends was old enough to drive. One of those trips was to Tuckerman's Ravine on Mount Washington, New Hampshire. "I almost broke my fool neck," Walt said in a 1953 article in the *New Haven (CT) Register*.

Walt also traveled to the Berkshires in Massachusetts and northwest Connecticut and visited many local ski hills. His travels would take him to Mohawk Mountain, where he skied the first trails created by the Civilian Conservation Corps in the late 1930s. Later, he also traveled to Vermont, looking for the best mountain for a future ski resort development.

Halfway across the world, Walt's future wife was also skiing. It was a passion she first experienced in Japan and would pursue until age eighty-one.

ONE BORN IN JAPAN, THE OTHER IN CONNECTICUT

Walt was born May 2, 1919, in New Haven, Connecticut, the first son of Henry and Meta Schoenknecht, owners of a fifteen-acre plant nursery and vegetable garden off Laurel Street in East Haven, Connecticut.

Henry Gustav Robert Schoenknecht was born in Connecticut on August 31, 1883; his wife, Meta Schumann, was born in Germany in 1884. U.S. Census records show that Meta immigrated to the United States in 1904. She met Henry while visiting relatives on the Connecticut shoreline, home to many German immigrants.

Carol Lugar said her grandmother was the oldest of a dozen siblings and the first to immigrate to the United States. Shortly after arriving in New York City, she took a job as a seamstress. "She would work to establish residency and save enough money to send back home for the next sibling to come over. She is credited with doing some of the work on Alice Roosevelt's wedding dress." Alice Roosevelt was the eldest daughter of President Theodore Roosevelt. Alice married U.S. Representative Nicholas Longworth in the East Room of the White House on February 17, 1906.

"Henry was good with his hands and tended to the garden and the landscaping," according to a December 2002 *Skiing Heritage* magazine article. "Meta raised chickens and had an egg route." Henry also listed his occupation as "machinist" and worked in a box company in New Haven, according to the 1930 census.

Walt's parents would live to see their son achieve his dream of opening the Mohawk Mountain ski area in Cornwall, Connecticut, and the Mount Snow resort in Vermont. Henry died in 1965 and Meta in 1980.

The last name Schoenknecht is a German name meaning "beautiful servant," according to igena.com, a DNA analysis company. The Schoenknecht surname is believed to have developed in the Middle Ages around 1300 for artisan craftsmen like carpenters and masons.

After he graduated from New Haven's Commercial High School in 1937, Walt planned to enter the Yale School of Forestry, but a business recession that year changed his direction. Instead, he worked at Yale as a bookkeeper. Walt's next plan was a trip to Alaska, later abandoned after his father persuaded him to take a job as an apprentice machinist at the National Folding Box Company in New Haven. His training as a

Walt Schoenknecht's 1937 class of 1937 yearbook photo. *New Haven Commercial High School class of 1937.*

machinist would prove valuable in his future ski business, giving him the skills to design and build ski tows, chairlifts and gondolas.

When he was twenty-one, Walt Schoenknecht was working as a tool and die maker at the Chance Vought aircraft plant in Stratford, Connecticut, according to his draft registration papers. The October 16, 1940 registrar's report listed his weight at 180 pounds and his height at six feet, four inches; he had brown hair and brown eyes.

Also working at the plant were three engineers: Wayne Pierce, Art Hunt and David Richey. In the late 1940s and early '50s, they worked with Schoenknecht to develop the world's first patented snow machine.

Margaret "Peg" Moss was born on August 5, 1917, in Karuizawa, Japan, the daughter of American engineer Robert Faulkner Moss and Sybil Howard Moss.

Peg, who was raised in Japan, was a graduate of the American School in Japan, where her father served as chairman for seventeen years. After graduating from the American School in the mid-1930s, she was given the opportunity to go to college in the United States.

Her father was president of the Oriental Steel Products Company in Tokyo, where he was responsible for building bridges, highways and public buildings in the Philippines and Japan. One of his biggest projects was the construction of the Yokohama Bridge over Tokyo Harbor.

According to his April 23, 1964 obituary in the *New York Times*, Robert Faulkner Moss arrived in Yokohama on June 18, 1910, to represent a

Peg Schoeknecht, *second from left*, stands between her aunt Esther and her father, Robert Faulkner Moss. Walt Schoenknecht is next to the pet collie. *Mohawk Mountain ski area.*

Youngstown, Ohio steel company. He organized the Oriental Steel Products Company with combined U.S. and Japanese capital to manufacture steel construction materials.

Because of his deep knowledge of the Japanese steel industry and having been a former leader of the prewar American colony in Japan, he served in an advisory capacity of the Office of Strategic Services during World War II. "Family history indicates he [Robert Faulkner Moss] was a bit of a spy," Carol Lugar said. "They will never, never convince me that they didn't know about Pearl Harbor."

Before the war, when the Moss children were heading to the United States to attend college, their ship stopped in Hawaii. There, State Department officials seized their passports and told them that they could not return to

Japan. "He was connected with some high-level people. He was friends with [General Douglas] MacArthur and there were a whole lot of people circling into his life. He was also well connected with high Japanese officials."

In 1940, Robert Moss returned to the United States. The Japanese empire had already been at war with China for three years. On December 7, 1941, there was the surprise Japanese attack on Pearl Harbor, Hawaii, which would plunge the United States into World War II.

Lugar said that her uncle Richard Moss returned to the United States a few years ago to attend a class reunion at Amherst College. "I picked him up at the train station and drove him to Amherst. We did have some discussions and, even then, [he] was evasive about what he [her grandfather] had been doing. Unofficially and in a vain way, [he] did admit that there was some spying."

When Peg was eighteen, her mother died at the age of forty-three. According to her daughter, Carol Lugar, she left Japan in the mid-1930s. Traveling by ocean liner, she arrived in California. There she earned a degree from Scripps College in Claremont, California. Before the war broke, she moved to New Haven, Connecticut, to study for her master's degree at the Yale School of Nursing.

While attending Yale, she would meet her future husband, Walt Schoenknecht.

BOTH WALT AND PEG SERVE IN WORLD WAR II

Because of his work at the Chance Voight aircraft plant in Stratford, Connecticut, Walt was not taken into the U.S. Marine Corps until 1944. He was trained as an aerial photographer, but the war ended before they could send him overseas.

In a 1961 *Sports Illustrated* article titled "Vermont's Phenomenal Snowman," Schoenknecht said that he chose to leave his job at the Stratford, Connecticut defense plant. "War clouds were gathering, and the handwriting was on the wall," he told writer Huston Horn. He said he was obliged to "move heaven and earth" to get out of his job at the aircraft plant and enlist in the Marine Corps.

His efforts were successful. The U.S. Department of Veterans Affairs lists Schoenknecht's enlistment date as June 6, 1944, and discharge on August 13, 1946. Schoenknecht said that when he was a marine stationed in Florida, he started a ski club. "We didn't go skiing exactly, we just thought about it," he said.

He was later transferred to Aircraft Engineering Squadron 12 at Virginia's Marine Base Quantico, south of Washington, D.C. While stationed there, Schoenknecht did manage to go skiing, but it required a thirty-three-hour trip. For that trip, he would take a 7:00 p.m. train from Washington, arriving at 2:00 a.m. the next day in New Haven. He would then walk to his family's house in East Haven, Connecticut, get a few hours of sleep before driving to the Berkshires at sunrise. He would be ready when the rope tows opened at 9:00 a.m., ski until noon and then begin the return trip to his marine camp.

Because of those marathon ski trips, he was often late returning to base. He told *Sports Illustrated* that his tardiness caused the Marine Corps to reduce his rank from corporal to private. Lugar also said that he "was almost kicked out, definitely disciplined, for flying under a bridge in D.C."

Peg enlisted in the U.S. Army on July 20, 1942. She served in a Yale Medical Unit in the Pacific Theater. Fluent in Japanese, she was asked to question Japanese prisoners of war. She was discharged on December 7, 1945, four years to the day after the Japanese attacked Pearl Harbor.

Records indicate that Walt and Peg were married in Elizabeth, New Jersey, where her father had settled after leaving Japan.

HOW WALT AND PEG PURSUED THEIR SKI DREAMS

In 1946, Walt and Peg were back home, married and free to pursue their dream of creating a ski area. "Long before he had secured his concession from the State Park and Forest Commission, Schoenknecht had flown over the area looking for skiable mountains and slopes which held the snow into the spring," according to a January 2, 1948 *Hartford (CT) Courant* article. "Mohawk's north and northwest descents had been in his mind and had provided his dream of a ski development for 10 years."

With interest in skiing growing in postwar America, Schoenknecht sensed an opportunity to create a ski area that would appeal to returning GIs and their "baby boom" children. "There was simply no one around astute enough to guess what was happening to the sport," recalled Schoenknecht in the 1961 *Sports Illustrated* article. Schoenknecht said that his ski area would be more accessible and appeal to both novices and experts. It was a notion out of step with a sport that was somewhat elitist at the time.

Mohawk was the only ski trail when Walt Schoenknecht got a lease in 1947 to develop a ski area. The chairlift was installed for the 1960–61 season. *Mohawk Mountain ski area.*

Often overlooked in most histories of Mohawk Mountain is Peg Schoenknecht. Likely it was because in that time decades ago, men were the "head of the house" and the "breadwinner" of the family. Many women stayed at home to raise the family; few, unlike Peg as a nurse, had professional careers. "Walt was an entrepreneur and ski industry pioneer and Peg was very much his partner; the 'woman behind the man,'" according to her 2008 obituary. "She helped him build and run Mohawk Mountain in Cornwall, which opened in 1947, and Mount Snow in Vermont in 1954. She had good business sense and was in many ways responsible for the success of both resorts. Much of the time, she ran Mohawk Mountain as Walt forged ahead with Mount Snow."

The Schoenknechts' marriage came at the cusp of a skiing boom that would explode in the mid-1960s and continue for twenty years. New areas were created to meet the growing demand of skiers. Many of those postwar areas were built by returning World War II veterans like the Schoenknechts.

"He decided that skiing was a good thing to do, something that he taught himself to do and enjoyed," his daughter, Carol Lugar, said in a 2012 interview with the Cornwall, Connecticut Historical Society. "He did a lot of research and found that this was one of the snowier areas of the state. And Mohawk being the third-highest peak in the state. He felt it had some potential. It was also enhanced by the fact that, at that time, the Appalachian Trail ran across the top. It had the trail and the shelters that came with the trail and some infrastructure. In addition to that, the CCC in the '30s had cut some 'touring trails' for skiing at the base of the mountain that we still use," Lugar added.

"Mohawk already had one ski trail, when the Schoeknechts came," according to a January 2, 1948 *Hartford (CT) Courant* article. "The trail was constructed several years ago by the CCC, but it was a hardy sportsman who made the climb which came before the downhill run."

TEST RUN AT MASSACHUSETTS' BRODIE MOUNTAIN

After Walt and Peg Schoenknecht were married, the couple honeymooned at a small rope tow ski area they leased at Brodie Mountain in northwest Massachusetts during the 1946–47 ski season. The area was south of the much larger Brodie Mountain ski area in the "Irish Alps," which would become a popular destination from the mid-1960s to early 2000s.

Many longtime skiers fondly remember the bigger Brodie's St. Patrick's Day party that included Irish music and dancers dressed as leprechauns. Shamrock images were painted in the snow, Irish whiskey flowed and bountiful corned beef dinners were served. Brodie also arranged for Irish priests to celebrate Mass in many of its pubs inside the lodge.

One of the first things Walt and Peg Schoenknecht did at Brodie was to install two new rope tows. The area was leased from a colorful character named Gregory Makaroff, known to some locals as the "Mad Russian," according to the *Berkshire Eagle*.

The small ski area began in the 1930s when Makaroff gave skiers permission to use the Brodie Mountain Trail that descended onto his property from the mountain's 2,600-foot summit. It soon became one of the most popular ski trails in Massachusetts's Berkshire County.

Makaroff, born in Russia in 1891, learned the cabinet trade as a boy and worked in steel mills in India before coming to the United States in the early twentieth century. "He served with the Army in Mexico before World War I, was kicked by a horse and suffered a back injury that bothered him for the rest of his life," according to an article in the *North Adams (MA) Transcript* that announced his death on July 13, 1949.

Makaroff, who moved to New Ashford, Massachusetts, in 1919, did work inlaying mother of pearl in cabinetry and other items. He established the Brodie Mountain ski tow in the mid-1930s, which he owned until he left the area in 1947.

The "Mad Russian" title may have come from a number of incidents, including one on February 21, 1944, when he was arrested after an argument at his rope tow. "He was arrested last night on a warrant sworn out by Benjamin Robinson of Pittsfield, who charges that during an argument over use of a ski tow, Makaroff grabbed his arm and tried to choke him and finally picked up a wrench in a threatening gesture," the *Transcript* reported.

Makaroff also sought restraining orders against the competing Brodie Mountain Sports Center, accusing people using the center of trespassing on his ski trails. He also got a court order that prevented the Sports Center from using Brodie in its name. Makaroff was also known to deflate the car tires of skiers whom he suspected of not paying for tow lift tickets.

He also had an outdoor dining room at his home near the Brodie ski area. The *Transcript* reported that every winter, Makaroff would use 150 pounds of suet to feed birds from three nearby towns "to satisfy his feathered guests, who are blue-jays, woodpeckers of four species and chickadees," the article stated. "They eat just outside his dining room window and he swears they know him, and talk to him when he is in the woods."

The Schoenknechts' first experience of running a ski area—and dealing with Makaroff—was a financial disaster. "We learned a lot that winter, but the crowds weren't as big as we hoped because it was a good winter and ski tows farther south got most of the business," Walt said of the Brodie season.

Schoenknecht also claimed that Makaroff took a big portion of the area's revenue. Schoenknecht later told ski writer Lee Leahy that "I lost my shirt."

In a 1979 interview with the *Berkshire Eagle*, Schoenknecht recalled, "Gregory had a five-strand barbed wire fence [to stop trespassers] that had to be taken down—this took some persuading. I learned more about the Russians from Gregory. He had a perpetual motion machine that looked like a butter churn, and it was all hush, hush. He was extremely skilled. He really had cancer but didn't want anyone to know about it."

CONNECTICUT GRANTS LEASE
FOR MOHAWK MOUNTAIN SKI AREA

Returning to Connecticut, Walt and Peg Schoenknecht had bigger and better plans. Knowing that Connecticut forestry officials were eager to establish the state's first large ski area, he came up with a long-term lease proposal for a private/public partnership to develop the Mohawk Mountain ski area.

In March 1947, Connecticut governor James L. McConaughy, a Cornwall, Connecticut resident, signed a State Park and Forest Commission lease giving twenty-eight-year-old Walt Schoenknecht permission to develop a ski area on Mohawk's northwest slope, known as the Pinnacle. The fee for the lease for one hundred acres was $100 per year.

The lease allowed Walt Schoenknecht to carve new trails, install rope tows and build warming shelters, parking lots and entrance roads. It also allowed the sale of lift tickets and food; alcohol was prohibited.

In a January 1970 ski column in the *Bridgeport (CT) Post*, Ken Maloney wrote that his newspaper had "indirectly played a role" in the creation of the Mohawk Mountain ski area. "The *Post*'s then editor-in-chief, the late

Along with rope tows, T-bars were used to carry skiers to the top hill at many early ski areas. *Mohawk Mountain ski area.*

George C. Waldo, was chairman of the State Parks and Forest Commission, who backed the idea of a ski area development. You may be surprised to know that skiers that first winter at Mohawk didn't have very far to go for ski conditions, since *The Post* carried them on page one."

EARLY SKI HILLS IN CONNECTICUT

Before Mohawk opened in 1947, there were no big ski areas in Connecticut. The state's three steepest ski trails in existence at the time were in state parks and forests, including the original Mohawk trail carved in 1939. At Haystack Mountain in Norfolk, there was a 30-foot-wide, half-mile-long trail with a 450-foot vertical drop. And in the Tunxis State Forest in Hartland, there was a three-quarter-mile trail with a 700-foot vertical drop. All these trails were never groomed, and none had any tows.

A January 5, 1948 ski report described the conditions in the state forests as fair because of mild weather. "State Forester Raymond E. Keinholz said there is about eight inches of granular snow at the Mohawk forest run; trail conditions are good only in spots. At Tunxis state forest the trail is covered with about ten inches of granular snow topped by a breakable crust. At Haystack Mountain State Park conditions are about the same. All roads leading to the trails have been cleared."

Connecticut also had many local ski hills run by towns, ski clubs and local farmers. Most of the areas were tiny; they had small vertical drops and a few rope tows often powered by old car or tractor engines. These small ski areas were very important because they served as a kind of nursery for novice skiers. The people who learned there would later go on to ski with their children at the larger areas created during the skiing boom in the late 1950s to the mid-1980s.

Snowsports writer and meteorologist Jeremy Davis's New England Lost Ski Area Project (https://www.nelsap.org/ct/ct.html) lists fifty-nine early ski hills in Connecticut, including Besse Park in Torrington, Bronson's Hill in Washington, the YMCA Camp Jewel in Colebrook, Sweetheart Hill in Collinsville, the Mad Hatter Ski Slopes in Danbury, Rattlesnake Mountain in Somers and Sharon Mountain in Sharon.

Ski club–operated hills were located in Thomaston, Hartford, Manchester, Bristol and Bloomfield. Skiing on those slopes depended on natural snow, and they were open a short time in winter, mostly in January and February.

Another ski hill in Winsted was Laurel Hill, formerly the prewar Silver Streak run, which had 1,300- and 800-foot tows.

Other popular ski hills were Bethany Ridge, with one of the first ski tows in the state, and Durham, with a one-thousand-foot tow that served intermediate and expert skiers.

The Simsbury Ski Club Hill, started in 1936, claimed to be the first ski hill in Connecticut. Priscilla Smith (Bourgeois) Scheiner, who lived near the Simsbury ski hill, posted on the New England Lost Ski Area Project website that the "original tow, copied from the Whitney ski slope in Vermont, consisted of a half-mile of Otis elevator cable and a Chevrolet motor. A year later, the club replaced the tow with a 1931 Buick, purchased for $41 from Duane Clement, who had retrieved the car from the bottom of Lake Congamond [in Suffield, Connecticut]."

Five days before the Mohawk Mountain ski area opened on December 26, 1947, the *Hartford (CT) Courant* published a ski guide that highlighted New England areas within 150 miles from Hartford. "Those vigorous stalwarts who don't mind getting up very early in the morning and driving home very late at night can make many of the places mentioned in a day," the article noted.

SLOW ROADS TO BIGGER MOUNTAINS FARTHER NORTH

In 1947, there were no interstate highways with sixty-five-mile-per-hour speed limits. One major road was Route 5 alongside the Connecticut River, traveling from Connecticut to the Canadian border. Route 7 in Massachusetts and Route 22 in New York were good two-lane roads to take if you were heading to ski areas in western Massachusetts, Vermont and eastern New York. Both highways ran through numerous towns and villages, with numerous stop signs and traffic lights often increasing travel times.

In Mohawk Mountain's first few years of operation, the closest big ski areas—those with vertical drops of more than one thousand feet— were in western Massachusetts, including Catamount in Egremont, Beartown Mountain in Lee, the G-Bar-S Dude Ranch (now Butternut) in Great Barrington and Thunder Mountain (now Berkshire East) in Charlemont.

Other western Massachusetts ski hills highlighted in a December 21, 1947 *Hartford Courant Magazine* article by Richard A. Stevens included:

- The Bousquet Ski Grounds in Pittsfield. "This 'Ski Bunnies Paradise' offers more than 100 acres of play area. Two rope tows have been added this year, bringing the total now operating to 10, thus providing facilities for all. Sophisticated experts will find it poor skiing except under ideal snow conditions."
- The "Chickley Alp," which had eight tows near North Adams, "offers excellent open slope conditions as well as three and one-half miles of trails with good snow conditions."
- The "King of the Bay State ski areas is probably Mt. Greylock, embracing as it does the highest peak in the Commonwealth. The Thunderbolt trail, located on the northeast shoulder, is nearly one and one-half miles long, with a 2,050-feet vertical drop. Another outstanding trail is the 'Cheshire Harbor,' two and one-half miles long, six to 20 feet wide, vertical drop 2,000 feet. Both are for experts."
- Other western Massachusetts areas mentioned included "Sheep's Hill" in Williamstown, 1,400-foot vertical drop; "Black Panther" in Huntington, 1,200 feet; "Sunnyside Ranch" in Westfield, 1,000 feet; Blanford, 1,000 feet; and Mount Wachusett in Princeton, 1,000 feet.
- Jiminy Peak in Hancock, near the New York border, featured a 2,300-foot T-bar lift, the first in Massachusetts, as well as a rope tow serving open slopes.

It took more time to travel to the bigger and steeper ski areas in Vermont and New York. With no high-speed interstate highways in the late 1940s and early '50s, a few days were needed to enjoy ski areas in the White Mountains of New Hampshire and Maine.

"Vermont offers the skier of any degree of excellent conceivable fare," Stevens wrote. "Trails for all types of skiers, excellent accommodations, cafeterias, lifts, rope tows, repair shops and excellent ski instruction."

WHY MOHAWK MOUNTAIN WAS CHOSEN AS A SKI AREA

Walt Schoenknecht told the *Litchfield (CT) Enquirer* in October 1947 that it took several years of study—and dreaming—to find the best location for a large Connecticut ski area. Mohawk Mountain, he said, "lies directly in the

This map shows the location of Northeast ski areas in the winter of 1950–51. *From* SKI Magazine, *December 1950.*

middle of the snow belt which runs into [Canada's] Laurentian [Mountains] and this particular mountain is so situated that it is protected from the sun and wind." He also said that several trails could be developed, all of which would have one starting place.

Initial work on the ski area began in February 1947. With the help of his father, Henry; his wife, Peg; and many volunteers, trail work started along the existing Mohawk trail, built in 1939.

"The earliest structure here was what we now refer to as the Pine Lodge, which is an old building that's midway up the mountain," Carol Lugar told the Cornwall Historical Society. "This was the first base lodge up there. You had to hike up to it. The ticket office was down at the bottom. Our little ski patrol building was part ski patrol building and part ticket office at that point."

The Pine Lodge served both as a ski lodge and the family's home. An attached building had a ski shop, a first-aid clinic and day care for kids. "My grandfather [Henry Schoenknecht] would help with things," Lugar said. "Among other things, most of the trees, the specimen trees that are still here—unfortunately not a lot of them are left, we lost a lot of them in the [1989] tornado—came from my grandfather Henry's nursery at his home in East Haven. There's some stonework around. The fireplace at Pine Lodge is stone that my grandfather cut at his home in East Haven."

Members of the New Haven Ski Club, the Sterling House Ski Club of Stratford and similar groups from Litchfield and Hartford counties helped with seeding and smoothing the freshly cut trails.

Walt Schoenknecht told the *Litchfield (CT) Enquirer* that the work on the ski area "was under the enthusiastic eye of thousands of Connecticut skiers who at times have come by the busload to hand pick the trails of stones and who have done a lot of the cutting and cleaning up the area."

Two of the rope tows used earlier by the Schoenknechts at Brodie were moved to Mohawk Mountain. Four more were added, including three that went to the top of the hill. Before the 1947–48 ski season began, six rope tows were added—four faster ones for experienced skiers and two slower tows (moving at seven miles per hour) for novices.

The six trails for the first season were longer, steeper trails for intermediate skiers and "cradle slopes" for beginners. Some of the trails were eighty feet wide and three-quarters of a mile long. The vertical drop was more than six hundred feet. "These are not just converted cow pastures," Schoenknecht said, "but will give the starter ample opportunity to learn and to learn safely."

Royal Whitman, a *Hartford Times* reporter, visited Mohawk a month before it opened on December 26, 1947. "Being a skier himself [Walt Schoenknecht]

The Pine Lodge was open for Mohawk's first season in 1947–48. It served as a lodge, a ski shop and the family's home. *Mohawk Mountain ski area.*

has tailor-made his trails to suit the desires of all grades of skiers. Long smooth open slopes and wide, well-planned trails afford the novice and intermediate a wealth of skiing pleasure. The advanced intermediate and expert will be reminded of [New Hampshire's] Cannon Mountain smoothly manicured trails for Schoenknecht has provided trails with up to 30-degree slopes and close to a mile of a downhill run."

Before the first season began, the Schoenknechts' daughter, Carol, was born on December 9, 1947. Carol Schoenknecht Lugar would later become the Mohawk Mountain ski area co-owner/president and lead it into the twenty-first century. Schoenknecht and her mother, Peg, would later shepherd Mohawk through some of its toughest times, including the death of Walt Schoenknecht in 1987 and devastating tornados in 1989.

Walt Schoenknecht said in a 1947 interview that when Carol reached one year old, "I'll put her on a pair of skis, take her to a hill and shove her off—it's the only way to learn."

On the eve of Mohawk's opening, Schoenknecht told the Associated Press that his ski area was not dependent on heavy snowfalls. "The trails unlike those in deep snow country are planned for good skiing with a four-inch

Left: A young Carol Schoenknecht with likely her first pair of skis outside the Pine Lodge. *Mohawk Mountain ski area.*

Below: Mohawk's first ski shop offered rental ski equipment and repairs. It was attached to the Pine Lodge. *Mohawk Mountain ski area.*

Opposite: An early ski map before Mohawk's first season shows trails named after Connecticut's Native American tribes. *Mohawk Mountain ski area.*

base. An 18-ton bulldozer ripped out every tree stump after the trails were cut on Mohawk and grass was planted to make the surface almost as smooth as a golf fairway." In preparation for the expected crowds of skiers, a dirt parking lot for 350 vehicles was cleared.

In the late fall of 1947, Connecticut newspapers gave readers a preview of the new Mohawk Mountain ski area. A November 30, 1947 article in the *Bridgeport (CT) Sunday Post* had the headline "State's Snow-Bowl a Skiers' Paradise" and "Winter Wonderland Created in the Mohawk State Forest."

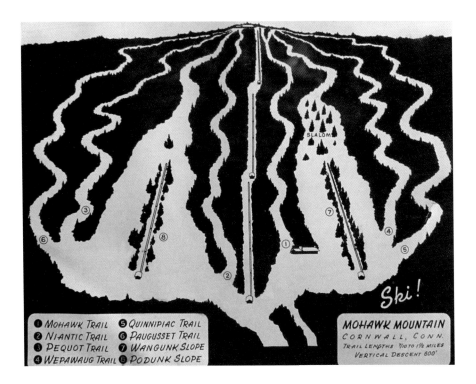

SLALOM

Ski!

❶ MOHAWK TRAIL ❺ QUINNIPIAC TRAIL
❷ NIANTIC TRAIL ❻ PAUGUSSET TRAIL
❸ PEQUOT TRAIL ❼ WANGUNK SLOPE
❹ WEPAWAUG TRAIL ❽ PODUNK SLOPE

MOHAWK MOUNTAIN
CORNWALL, CONN.
TRAIL LENGTHS 7/10 TO 1½ MILES
VERTICAL DESCENT 600'

Along with describing the trails and rope tows, *Hartford (CT) Courant* reporter Mary Darlington Taylor was impressed by the lodge. "But certainly, there is a lodge. A mighty fancy one, built of varicolored masonry block, with a sky-blue roof, snuggled under a grove of white pine like a remote, Alpine chalet."

Inside the lodge was a "food-bar," ski rental/repair shop and toilets. Next to the lodge was another small building "which promises to be the biggest hit of anything at Mohawk, outside of the trails....It is the baby pen where, under care of a registered nurse small fry can be parked while mamma joins papa on the trails and slopes."

Taylor wrote that "the place is more than a ski area. The lover of winter scenery will be enchanted with the intelligent way that Schoenknecht, a landscape gardener by hobby, has preserved the natural beauty, without sacrificing trail safety or efficiency."

An early ski map before Mohawk's first season showed that ski trails were initially named after Connecticut Native American tribes, including Niantic, Pequot, Wepawaug, Quinnipiac, Paugusset, Wangunk and Podunk. A contest was later held to have skiers name the ski trails.

A SNOWY OPENING DAY

After spending $45,000 on the project—the Schoenknechts' and their parents' money—the Mohawk Mountain ski area officially opened on December 26, 1947. It offered six trails, including the original Mohawk run, carved in 1939.

During its first day of operation, snow began to fall at Mohawk Mountain. It was the beginning of a major snowstorm that would bring the most snow seen in some areas, like New York City, since the Blizzard of 1888.

Snowfall in Connecticut ranged between twelve and twenty inches, according to a December 27, 1947 front-page story in *The Day* of New London, Connecticut: "Along the Merritt Parkway between Milford and the New York state line, hundreds of automobiles were stalled, some of them in drifts which topped five feet in places that were at least partially protected from high winds which helped hard pressed highway department crews in their efforts to keep the highways open.…More than 100 motorists were rescued from stalled cars on the parkway and taken to shelter in homes, gas stations and wherever the police could find room."

Six Connecticut residents died in that snowstorm, including Reverend William J. Dunn, the sixty-four-year-old pastor of St. James Church in Manchester. Police said that Dunn died of a heart attack while returning from a sick call at the home of a parishioner. Earlier, Father Dunn had helped shovel snow from the church's sidewalk and a grave.

While the snowstorm caused major delays, disruption and deaths, skiers nonetheless celebrated the snow and the chance to visit Connecticut's newest ski area.

By late morning on Saturday, December 27, 1947, the state transportation department said most highways were passable. One day during the 1947 Christmas/New Years week, more than 1,200 skiers showed up at Mohawk Mountain. Thanks to natural snowfall, Mohawk started its first season with a nearly 20-inch snow base.

A January 26, 1948 Associated Press article gave a positive review to the new ski area. "For years, New England neighbors from Maine to Massachusetts and the canny Canadians have been coining money from snow-covered slopes. Now in the Mohawk State Forest, Connecticut has its first skiing center capable of rivaling those to the north.…Skiing can be big business because skiers, although a hardy breed willing to brave sub-freezing temperatures and risk the chances of a broken limb, are essentially lazy. They love to slide down a hill, but they hate to climb back up. So much that they'll pay money to be towed."

Skiers on Mohawk's beginner slope. Thanks to natural snowfall, Mohawk started its first season with a nearly twenty-inch base. *Mohawk Mountain ski area.*

The price of being towed up the mountain, according to the article, was $2 per day and $1.50 for a half day. With a week's attendance at nearly 2,500, it "adds up to a lot of money," the unnamed author surmised. "Carve out trails on a small-sized mountain and rig up a method of hauling up skiers on the mountainside and you have the basis for a tidy business."

That "tidy business," however, did have some risks—lots of them. The first was the lack of snow to ski on. Walt Schoenknecht said that he and Peg spent most of their life savings to create the ski area. He called the ski business "a gamble." And with plenty of natural snow in the 1947–48 winter, that gamble paid off. Skiing that season continued to the end of March.

Schoenknecht said that he "had wonderful luck" in the first season. "A winter like this probably won't come again in years. We might as well be realistic about this."

OPTIMISM, THEN DISAPPOINTMENT
WITH NATURAL SNOWFALLS

After a first successful ski season, the owners of the Mohawk Mountain ski area were excited to offer new trails and rope tows for the 1948–49 ski season. A great sense of anticipation and optimism was in the air. The first season of 1947–48 netted a profit of nearly $10,000 on income of $47,300, according to the New England Ski Museum.

"Walt and Peg Schoenknecht, who dreamed Mohawk into its present skiable state, came back from a busman's tour of the West and brought with them ideas that they have adapted to the Cornwall area," the *Hartford (CT) Times* reported in an October 6, 1948 article. "The tows now have downhill shoots as you jump on, and downhill shoots as you climb off. That will do a great deal towards helping tow congestion and will help those who baffled by ropes."

A new section of the ski area for intermediate and expert skiers would open in Mohawk's second season. "This pitch, called the Boulder Bowl, is steep enough to make many a lad or lass wish for laminated wings," the *Times* reported. "The two trails cut into the new area have a vertical descent of 500 feet with a maximum grade of 30 degrees. Serviced by two tandem tows, the trails are wide [200 to 300 feet] and are scooped out in the center. The hollowing is a new idea and is expected to keep the trails well covered even though skied by heavy crowds. A cutback connects the two new trails, Wildwood and Timber, to the main area."

Opposite: The Timber trail has a vertical descent of five hundred feet, with a maximum grade of thirty degrees. *Mohawk Mountain ski area.*

Above: In the 1949–50 season, Mohawk added the Timber and Wildwood trails. The image shows a bulldozer on what appears to be the Timber trail. *Mohawk Mountain ski area.*

The article gushed with details of the new Laurel slope, which "is wide and excellent for practicing and schooling." Additional rope tows, a new sky-blue roof on the ski lodge and an outdoor, glassed-in terrace were among the improvements. Meg Mallory's *Hartford (CT) Times* article ended, "The entire area is now ready for the first snow."

Unfortunately for skiers, and Mohawk Mountain, there was very little natural snow. Walt Schoenknecht was desperately looking for a way to keep his ski area open. He had some unusual ideas of how to do that and was looking for people to help him.

BIRTH OF SNOWMAKING

Disappointments and, Finally, Success

WHO INVENTED THE SNOWMAKING MACHINE?

Several individuals took the first steps eventually leading to the development of the modern snowmaking machine. It was an invention that revolutionized how ski areas could survive and extend their seasons with little natural snow.

From the first successful method of grinding up tons of one-hundred-pound ice blocks to create a skiable, slippery surface in the early 1930s to the rudimentary snowmaking machines in the late 1940s and early 1950s, it was often a trial-and-error experiment with accidental discoveries.

Except for ski historians, few people know the names of Wayne M. Pierce, Arthur R. Hunt and David Richey, who were three aviation engineers in their twenties. They worked at a Stratford, Connecticut defense plant that built an airplane that would help end World War II. The three would later form the Tey Manufacturing Company and be granted the first U.S. patent for a snowmaking machine.

More may know Walt Schoenknecht, the avid skier and marine veteran who founded the Mohawk Mountain ski area in Cornwall, Connecticut, and the Mount Snow resort in West Dover, Vermont. Before opening those areas, he was intrigued by water sprayers that produced a fine mist, which protected delicate tobacco plants from freezing in the Connecticut River Valley, according to his daughter, Carol Lugar.

He wondered if a similar system, or other methods, could create "artificial snow" to keep ski areas open during stingy snow years. Today,

From left to right: Wayne Pierce, Dave Richey and Art Hunt with their early snowmaking machine in 1950. *New England Ski Museum.*

the name "artificial snow" is no longer used. The more accurate term is "machine-made snow."

While Schoenknecht did not directly invent the snowmaking machine, he was its first evangelist, spreading news of its game-changing benefits to many ski writers and members of northeastern ski clubs. His zeal, drive, promotion and innovations would garner national attention in such magazines as *LIFE* and *Sports Illustrated*.

More importantly, he brought together the key people who created, collaborated, tested and tinkered to install the first snowmaking system at Mohawk in 1950. They included Phil and Joe Tropeano, two brothers from Lexington, Massachusetts. Their business, Larchmont Farms Irrigation Company, would provide the water piping to help Schoenknecht and the Tey engineers create the snowmaking system. The Tropeanos would later acquire the snowmaking patent, and from 1958 to 1976, they marketed and installed snowmaking systems around the world. Larchmont would also help Mohawk expand its snowmaking coverage.

Likely the least-known name is Ray Wringer, a Canadian aviation engineer whom the *Guinness Book of World Records* credits with making the first artificial snow in the 1940s. "Their discovery was accidental while researching the formation of ice on jet engines. They sprayed water into a low-temperature wind tunnel in front of a jet engine, which proceeded to produce snow out

Joe Tropeano, *pictured*, and his brother Phil's business, Larchmont Farms Engineering, provided the water piping to help create Mohawk's first snowmaking system in 1950. *Larchmont Snowmaking.*

of its rear end," stated the record book. "They produced so much snow that the wind tunnel and engine had to be regularly shut off in order to clear away the snow. Uninterested in pursuing a commercial application, Ringer published his results in the scientific community which ultimately led to a US patent being granted to other researchers in 1954."

The New England Ski Museum's Chronology of Snowmaking states, "There was definite agreement within the skiing industry that manufactured snow was produced in Canada during the mid to late forties. During that period, the Canadians (and the British and Americans) were experimenting with de-icing equipment on airplanes....It was necessary to produce 'field' conditions at the testing facilities to properly determine the effectiveness of the numerous de-icing methods. Various nozzles were fabricated in an effort to generate freezing rain, fog, and sleet. The output from the nozzles was described in the literature as snow."

The nearly snowless winter of 1948–49 accelerated the search for other ways to help ski areas survive. Few knew at the time that people were already working behind the scenes to achieve that goal.

In a January 19, 1949 *Hartford Courant* article, Schoenknecht took a long view of the situation. "It's a hard year, but the operator who doesn't plan for this kind of thing is going to go under." He said that one year out of six is usually a bad ski year.

Schoenknecht said that the chief activity in January 1949 wasn't opening ski trails but rather fixing landslide damage caused by a 9.5-inch rainfall. Ever the optimist, he said, "It might have been a 100-inch snowfall." Yet the reality was that the New England ski business lost $4 million in the 1948–49 season; many hotels and inns were deserted, and three hundred ski lifts remained idle, the Associated Press reported.

Years later in 1953, Schoenknecht was asked by the *New Haven Register* about the earth's climate getting warmer. "Well, I was out at Glacier Park [in Montana] last summer and the glaciers were lengthening for the first time in years. Even if the earth is getting warmer it is a very slow process and I'm not too worried about it."

CRUSHED ICE:
FIRST SOLUTION FOR SNOW-STINGY WINTERS

Give credit to the Canadians, who were the first to use shaved ice for a ski jumping competition in 1934. "A novel experiment was attempted by the Toronto Ski Club 'Board of Strategy' when faced with the opening of their new jump with a major competition and no snow in sight," wrote Fred A. Hall in the *Canadian Ski Year Book*. "An excellent substitute for snow was shaved ice. They made arrangements with the University of Toronto skating rink to have their ice planer work overtime. Several trucks were employed to haul pulverized ice to the jump, a distance of about four miles. Seventy-five tons were cut and delivered in a few hours. This was sufficient to cover the entire hill from tower to outrun, with about six or eight inches on the landing slope."

Hall added, "It was from ten to twenty percent faster than dry snow, as jumps made that day were comparatively longer. The total cost of 'manufacturing' the snow was about $80, or approximately $1 per ton. This was for trucking alone as the cutting was done for free."

Also in 1934, ski jumpers competed on crushed ice at Bear Mountain, on the west bank of the Hudson River in Orange County, New York. "From the 1930s, Bear Mountain was the main ski jumping center in the U.S.," according to the Ski Jumping Hall Archive. The site was also considered for the 1932 Winter Olympics, although that was later given to Lake Placid, New York. Ski jumping competitions were held there through 1990.

In December 1937, crushed ice was also used at the Boston Garden Ski Show. "The snow is really ground ice ground into corn snow likeness from regular commercial blocks," a *Boston Globe* article stated. "It is ground and blown out through a special machine developed by the Link Belt Company for icing refrigerator freight cars and takes about 13 hours and a little over 100 tons of ice for the first 'coating.' Thereafter, 10 to 15 tons a day is needed to keep the hill in condition."

IN A WARM 1949 SUMMER, PEOPLE WERE FASCINATED BY "ARTIFICIAL SNOW"

As the 1940s were coming to a close, most people knew very little about using crushed ice as a substitute for snow. In 1949, there were other things on their minds, including the second "Red Scare," when the FBI named celebrities as reported Communist Party members, the first test of a nuclear bomb by the Soviet Union and the formation of the People's Republic of China.

With the Cold War atmosphere heating up, a photo spread in the warm summer of 1949 may have provided some welcome relief in newspapers. With a daily circulation of 52,846,000, newspapers were the main source of information in 1949, according to the Pew Research Center. By 2022, U.S. newspaper circulation (print and digital) had fallen to 20.9 million.

Many newspapers ran two photos taken in Cleveland, Ohio. One showed a kid on a sled and another a crew blowing chopped ice onto grass. "It's snow, honest to goodness snow falling in Cleveland on July 28 with the temperature at 93," the caption read. "And it didn't take Jackie Steiner, 7, more than a minute to grab his sled and his ear-flap cap and go sledding in the stuff."

The article said the snowmaking machine belonged to a Cleveland ice company whose officials came up with a way to save lawns during heat waves. "They put chemical fertilizer in 300-pound ice cakes, haul them to the lawn, grind the ice into snow and blow it on the grass. The snow melts to give the grass a good soaking and make it greener. The snow machine also blows pure ground ice on perishable produce in freight cars."

The Council Bluffs *Iowa Nonpareil* reported on March 7, 1949, "C.A. Swanson and sons have installed a new snow-making machine at its plant capable of turning out eight tons of snow in 24 hours"—not for skiing, but rather for its "new poultry cooling process."

LACK OF NATURAL SNOW CRIPPLE AREAS, SKI MANUFACTURERS

Canadian aviation engineer Ray Ringer did not seek a patent after snow was produced in a wind tunnel in the mid-1940s. Instead, he wrote a research paper that likely caught the attention of Wayne Pierce and the two other Connecticut engineers.

In a March 16, 1950 article in the *Hartford Courant*, Tey president Art Hunt said that he was aware of the wind tunnel snow. "To the best of my knowledge we are the first to convert water to snow in an open field." He added, "The process has been in large experimental stations such as Wright Field in Ohio" and other aviation test facilities.

The three engineers worked at the Chance Voight aircraft plant in Stratford, Connecticut. The plant, a Sikorsky division of United Aircraft, built 7,829 Corsairs at the Stratford plant, according to the Connecticut Air & Space Center.

"The Corsair F4U entered combat in 1943 and gave the Allied naval aviators a winning edge against their opponents," according to the National World War II Museum. "Renowned for its speed [up to four hundred miles per hour], ruggedness and firepower, the Corsair excelled as both a fighter and an attack aircraft in support of ground forces." The Corsairs also dropped heavy bombs and fired the first missiles from fighter planes.

With World War II coming to an end, the aircraft plant was developing some postwar products. One of those products—the Metallite ski—came from a wood-metal laminate material initially designed for the Corsair's gull-shaped wings. The smooth surface panels eliminated the need for rivets and spot welding, thus reducing turbulence on the aircraft.

"Several of the Chance Voight engineers who were caught up in the thrills of skiing, thought the Metallite process could be incorporated into the design of skis and suggested it as a consumer product. With a tentative go-ahead, we made about 1,000 pairs of skis and shipped them to well-known skiers all over the world for testing," Hunt wrote in

In 1947, Art Hunt, Wayne Pierce and Dave Richey formed Tey Manufacturing in Milford, Connecticut. Its headquarters was removed in 1958 for turnpike construction. *New England Ski Museum.*

a 1990 *Ski Area Management* article. "The survey questionnaire that the skiers returned to us said they were terrific. Unfortunately, the Navy and the Marines revealed other ideas for Chance Voight and the skis were dropped in favor of more Corsairs."

Also working at the Stratford plant at that time was Schoenknecht, the tall, lanky Connecticut native who became friends with Pierce. Pierce, a Massachusetts Institute of Technology graduate, was the plant's chief of design operations. Like Schoenknecht, all the engineers were avid skiers.

In 1947, Hunt, Pierce and Richey decided to leave the aircraft plant and start their own business, the Tey Manufacturing Company. The company's name came from the final letters of their last names. The company's headquarters was located on Ford Street in Milford. It was removed to make way for construction of the Connecticut Turnpike in 1958.

"Wayne M. Pierce Jr., David M. Richey and I were all in our mid-twenties and thought we could do more creative engineering and manufacturing," Hunt wrote.

Tey's aluminum ski didn't sell well because the 1948–49 winter had little natural snow. The surplus skis were often given away as prizes in Mohawk costume contests. *Mohawk Mountain ski area.*

Their ski design was slightly different from Chance Voight's patented Metallite ski. Pierce developed his idea of making an aluminum ski with a hollow interior and three layers of metal bonded together. Production of the ski, named the ALU-60, began in the summer of 1947. A pair of these skis can still be seen at the main lodge of the Mohawk Mountain ski area. The silver-colored skis are located near the lodge's ceiling, attached to one of the lodge's wooden beams.

A 1948 advertisement for the laminated metal skis promised, "They won't splinter, warp and they don't need waxing." Another ad called the ALU-60 "the most revolutionary improvement in ski equipment history." The company also produced Tey Tape, a plastic film it said "has excellent adhesive quality and eliminates lacquering" or waxing.

The metal skis weren't cheap, selling for $35 a pair. In 1948, a pair of hickory skis cost $9.94, and ones with metal edges were $14.94. An ad for the Alling Rubber Company in West Haven and Hartford, Connecticut, offered a complete package of wooden skis, bamboo poles, metal bindings and ski boots for $27.50.

The "revolutionary" aluminum ski didn't sell well because the 1948–49 winter had little natural snow. The company was left with a warehouse of unsold metal skis. For years, Schoenknecht would use surplus ALU-60 skis as prizes in Mohawk ski competitions and costume contests. "We hadn't sold many skis that season and were practically out of business," Hunt wrote.

Schoenknecht was in the same predicament—little snow would ruin his business. He decided to use a process that was first used at ski jumping sites years earlier.

1950: CRUSHED ICE HELPS KEEP MOHAWK SKI AREA OPEN

The 1949–50 season started with little natural snow on the ground. "We were getting desperate," Schoenknecht told the *New York Times* in February 1985. "Then it dawned on me how they make snow out of crushed ice at a ski jump in Salisbury, which is 15 miles away. And then I thought, if they can do it, why can't we?"

The Salisbury Winter Sports Association was able to run a ski jumping competition on January 8, 1950, after spreading 120 tons of crushed ice on its jump and landing area. Schoenknecht would take it a few runs down

The Salisbury Winter Sports Association was able to run a ski jumping competition on January 8, 1950, after spreading 120 tons of crushed ice. *New England Ski Museum.*

Two rented chipping machines pulverized the ice and blew it out a hose to a distance around fifty feet. *New England Ski Museum.*

Salisbury's slope after the jumping competition was over. He said that if the mild weather continued, he would use crushed ice on Mohawk's ski trails.

"It's the first time the idea has ever been attempted on such a large scale and I'll probably lose $1,000 or more on it. But it would still be a shot in the arm for skiing. Mild weather and the lack of snow are making people forget about skiing," Schoenknecht told the *Times.*

The grinding of the ice came from two rented chipping devices used for railroad cars in New Haven, Connecticut. Crushed ice kept produce fresh while being shipped. The machine was pulled by a tractor to various sections along ski trails, where the ice would be pulverized and blown out a four-inch hose to a distance of up to fifty feet.

Getting tons of ice in 1950 was not a problem. While many people had already switched from iceboxes to refrigerators, some icehouses were still in business. One of them was the Economy Ice Company in Torrington.

In an interview with the *American Ski Annual and Skiing Journal* (1950–51), Schoenknecht said, "Right after New Year's [1950], Frank Ellis, head of our Ski School, and I talked the idea over. I started checking equipment, ice, and

Walt Schoenknecht, *center*, and ski school director Frank Ellis watch pulverized ice being blown on Mohawk ski trails in January 1950. *New England Ski Museum.*

the weatherman on forecasts for the weekend. Great heaps of ice started appearing by Wednesday night, and by Thursday morning we found the blower was pulverizing the ice and blowing out its great plume of powder. Three nights and four days round the clock steadily, the ice trucks rolled, and the crusher roared."

He continued, "By Saturday, we had a slope over a quarter-mile long and two tows ready for use. The skiers really came out; comments were many and varied, but favorable. The snow itself was like a fast dry corn, packed well and stayed on the hill nicely."

Between January 18 and January 21, 1950, "the true genius of Walt Schoenknecht surfaced," Nils Ericksen wrote in May 1980 article in *Ski Area Management*. "He located 500 tons of ice in Torrington, 11 miles from Mohawk. At the end of four very long days, using 27 trucks, he was able to consume all the ice given him [besides at this point someone dropped some ice tongs in the ice crusher and stopped the operation]. Not enough trails were covered, so another 200 tons were located [in New Milford] and this allowed three tows to operate."

Schoenknecht told the *New York Times*, "Just as expected, the blades inside the crusher sliced the ice to bits and then sent it out to the slope as real good powder. It was good skiing, and it was also the beginning of a new era."

Schoenknecht told Michael Strauss, a former *Palm Beach Daily News* sports editor, "It was a great idea. We attracted a great crowd for that weekend's cake walk. But we had to give it up. It turned warm in two days. The ice melted. It was like water going down the drain. The experiment was too expensive to try again."

Besides the many lift tickets sold, there was a greater benefit: free national publicity. The *New York Daily News*, with a daily circulation of 2 million in 1950, ran five photos of the crushed ice skiing on its back page. The headline for the photo spread was "The Iceman Cometh," likely taken from the title of the then popular play written by Eugene O'Neill.

"Word of what we were doing got around quickly, and in a couple of days we had crews from the old Pathe Newsreel and Warner Brothers shooting film that was shown all over the country," Schoenknecht told the *Times*. He

In January 1950, more than seven hundred tons of ice blocks were pulverized and spread on Mohawk ski trails. Many skiers showed up, but the biggest benefit was national publicity. *New England Ski Museum.*

also said that Mohawk's skiing on crushed ice probably made half the front pages in the Northeast.

The *Bridgeport Post* ran a front-page photo of the operation on January 22, 1950, with the caption, "Here's how the snow-blitzed Mohawk Mountain, Friday and yesterday, answered to many a skier's prayer. Nearly 500 tons of ice were pulverized and blown on slopes and trails to make the area in Cornwall into a little snow oasis in the midst of a desert of bare ground that has had winter sports enthusiasts in the dumps this year—and how! An additional inch of heaven-sent powder, yesterday, helped the human snow-makers with the task."

The crushed ice on Mohawk's ski trails was the beginning of Walt's rise as a different breed of ski pioneer, one who not only took risks but also dared to make changes on how ski areas were operated and promoted.

Ski writer I. William Berry wrote that Schoenknecht "had a zealot's belief coupled with a hyperactive spirit and a snake-oil salesman's soul. The fact that he was six-foot-nine, skinny as a ski, with a rapid-fire delivery and dark-black snapping eyes that made him the terror of the ski club circuit didn't hurt either. The skeptics tried and became converts, and they came back again with their friends."

"UNDER THE SHROUD OF SECRECY": SNOWMAKING TESTS AT MOHAWK

While the first public announcement of a successful snow machine was made in March 1950, Nils Ericksen, a *Ski Area Management* writer, said that testing of a prototype device at Mohawk Mountain came earlier.

"Three friends of Walt's—Art Hunt, Wayne Pierce and Dave Richey—who had skied on Walt's snow, approached him the next winter ['49–'50] with an idea. They had formed the Tey Manufacturing Co. after the war in Milford, Connecticut, and were manufacturing aluminum skis. But they faced the same problem as Walt and other operators: the unpredictability of natural snowfall. Thus, under a shroud of secrecy, during December 1949, they brought one of their original snowmaking prototypes to Mohawk Mountain and actually produced the first documented machine-made snow for skiing."

An editorial note at the bottom of the article stated, "A great deal of credit used in [Ericksen's] 'History of Snowmaking' [article] goes to Bill Walsh, of Manchester, New Hampshire, who was one of the first sales engineers to concentrate solely on snowmaking systems. Also, Wayne Pierce and Art Hunt, willingly dredged up details and background on the very important early stages of snowmaking development."

Walsh, who grew up in East Hampton, Connecticut, was also a chemical engineer and a pioneer in the snowmaking industry. According to his obituary, he held several patents on dual-fluid atomization nozzles. He died on May 19, 2023, three weeks before his 102nd birthday.

Carol Lugar, Walt's daughter, also believes that tests of the first snowmaking machine at Mohawk were before 1950. The tests were conducted by the Tey engineers and, later, two Massachusetts brothers from Larchmont Farms Irrigation, who installed the aluminum pipes for the system. Carol, who was just two years old at the time, said that her knowledge comes from stories passed down by her family. "Knowing Dad, the experiments had been going on at least one year; he didn't have a lot of patience beyond that. He wanted it done and working. It probably cropped up as an idea one year, they played with for a year and then said, let's use this thing," Lugar said.

This early snow gun made by Larchmont Farms Engineering was used at Mohawk Mountain in the early 1960s. *Mohawk Mountain ski area.*

"To understand the whole thing better, you need to understand my dad. Everything was a means to an end. He didn't care how he got there. He didn't care who provided what or did what. These guys were all people he knew. Some of them were pre-war friends. Some of the people he had known living around Connecticut and were involved in the industrial stuff that was going on. And then, he would ask them for help."

She continued, "He never cared about the money; he wanted someone else to help him make this work. He never cared about the attention, until my mom got after him [around his 1979 Skiing Hall of Fame induction] that maybe he ought to get a grip on these kind of contributions" to snowmaking, Lugar said.

"Everybody thought dad was crazy. What I'm finding out now, he was just way ahead of his time. If you look at the things he tried to do with other ski areas. Everyone thought he was crazy with covered ski lifts and now look at them."

In 1962, Walt asked the Atomic Energy Commission for permission to use an atomic bomb to increase the vertical drop at the Mount Snow ski area. "The atomic bomb story irritates me most," Lugar said, "but there was history with that. People were asked for peaceful uses for it because they didn't understand what the ramifications were at the time."

She added, "This was just how dad's mind worked and that was key; he was thinking so far ahead that he had become known as kook."

MARCH 14, 1950:
SNOWMAKING MACHINE IS FRONT-PAGE NEWS

Tey kept the snowmaking machine secret until mid-March following a successful test at its Milford, Connecticut headquarters. In a 1990 article in *Ski Area Management*, former Tey president Art Hunt described the test:

On Monday morning on March 14 [1950], *Wayne* [Pierce] *came to work with an idea he had conceived over the weekend. He figured that a drop of water propelled through a below-freezing air temperature, would turn into a hexagonal crystal. Snowflakes are clusters of such crystals, so that would be snow.*

By Monday afternoon, we had assembled in our backyard the necessary equipment to attempt to create hexagonal crystals from water. We had a

Process Developed to Produce Artificial Snow

A new product—artificial snow—was announced today by the Tey Manufacturing corporation of Milford, ski equipment manufacturers. Corporation officers, including (left to right) Arthur R. Hunt, president; David M. Richey, treasurer, and Wayne M. Pierce, Jr., are shown with the system of pressurized hoses which produce snow for ski resorts when a balky Winter refuses to make the real stuff. (Story on Page Four)

The successful test of a snowmaking machine by engineers of the Tey Manufacturing Company made the front page of the *Bridgeport Post* on March 16, 1950. *New England Ski Museum.*

spray gun nozzle and a 10-horsepower compressor that had been used to paint the skis and I brought in some garden hose. We put everything inside a plywood box on a Christmas-tree stand. Fortunately, the weather, which had been unseasonably mild until that time, turned colder and the mist that exited the paint-spray nozzle turned into hexagonal crystals. The three of us took turns watching the thing all night and by the morning, we had an 18-inch pile of snow over a diameter of 20 feet.

Well, we were kind of conservative guys, but I admit, we were a little bit excited about making snow and so I called the local newspaper in New Haven. They sent a reporter out to see the pile of snow and the pictures got on the news wires. We were deluged with calls from all over. The Wall Street Journal *covered the story on the front page and [writer, world traveler and skier]* Lowell Thomas *announced it on his evening broadcast.*

We took the snowmaker over to Mohawk where we put in a temporary installation to test it and do some calculations.

Hunt said the lack of demand for their skis forced Tey engineers to research the fundamental characteristics of snow and its formation. The snowmaking machine was the end result of that study.

A front-page Associated Press article in Vermont's *Brattleboro Reformer* on March 16, 1950, announced that engineers had a way to coat hills with snow. "A system of manufacturing artificial snow for ski resorts when a balky winter refuses to make the natural stuff has been developed by a group of Milford, Connecticut engineers. The inventors claim it works—and have a backyard of 18 inches deep in snow to prove it when there's scarcely a trace elsewhere in town."

The article reported that the Tey engineers "had good reason for developing the system; they run a ski manufacturing outfit which has found business bad this year because a mild winter has left slopes bare."

Hunt said that a trial of the process convinced him the machine could produce a deep layer of snow on a ski slope overnight. He said a hose connected to the machine was turned on at the Milford plant at 8:00 p.m., and at 7:30 a.m. the next morning, the "artificial snow" was eighteen inches deep.

The Associated Press and United Press wire stories on the snow machine's initial success were picked up by many newspapers across the United States.

A *Boston Globe* article by reporter Pat Harty provided more details on how the device could radically change ski areas. "Man makes snow!!!," Harty wrote. "The Man…Arthur R. Hunt…engineer…ski maker, snow maker. Disgusted with New England's scarcity and the resultant lack of ski sales, Hunt, president of a Milford, Connecticut ski making firm, set about giving Mother Nature an assist. He is now marketing a machine that will provide a snow carpet that will provide a snow carpet of any desired depth, as long as the water supply holds out."

Hunt told the *Boston Globe* reporter, "We make our own clouds on the ground and seed them. We convert spring, lake, brook or lake water into snow—and every ski resort has amble water close at hand. We pump this water through our machine to make snow. What we produce is not frozen ice, but actual snowflakes just as they fall through the heavens."

Hunt in the March 16, 1950 *Boston Globe* article also described how the snowmaking system worked. The three-hose design had water flowing through a center nozzle, surrounded by two nozzles for streams of compressed air:

> *With the first frost of any winter we can immediately cover the slopes or trails with a blanket deep as needed. We could provide sufficient cover for*

the entire Nosedive trail at Mount Mansfield [in Stowe, Vermont] *that would cover the rocks and stumps deep enough to make the trail the safest in the country.*

The machinery would require a capital investment, but ski areas with large investments which lie idle while they wait for storms can be operating with our installation. And the upkeep is very low.

The necessary plant at a ski area would consist of a shed, the machine itself housed within it, a permanent water supply, and an air compressor, plus flexible pipe to be used to carry the water from the shed to the point where it would be used.

The water is piped into the spot where it is to be used and leaves the pipe as snow at the exit point. Super cooling of the water and proper exit pressure of the water and air mixture cause the formation of the snow.

We have built up an 18-inch cover of snow on a 30-foot by 60-foot area with a small experimental machine. We finished development of the machine six weeks ago.

Tey engineers plan to canvas Northeast ski resorts in the spring and summer and will prepare snowmaking system installations for resort operators "who wish to ensure next season's business against unpredictable weather conditions."

The *Wall Street Journal* wrote on June 21, 1950, "Art Hunt of the Tey Manufacturing Corp, president figures that the machine will cover a 100-foot wide and a half-mile long ski trail with six inches of the stuff [snow] in 12 hours. He expects to sell the blizzard maker for $15,000 to $25,000. His hottest prospect at the moment is Walt Schoenknecht, who had to grind up several tons of ice so he could use his 11 rope-tow ski area at Cornwall, Connecticut."

The news of a snow machine even spread to the Land Down Under. Australia's *South Coast Times* ran a story on May 22, 1950, with the headline "Artificial Snow for U.S. Skiers." The article said, "Skiers at winter resorts in the United States next winter may coast down slopes covered with artificial snow when there is no natural snow available. The white slippery surface will be produced by a new machine that has been developed in the United States."

SCHOENKNECHT "STUNT" OFFERS SKIING
ON PINE NEEDLES

Before the 1950–51 ski season began, Walt Schoenknecht hosted the Connecticut Ski Council's outing in early October. It was a day for socializing, cooking food on open fires, horseshoes, badminton, archery and skiing. Although there wasn't any natural snow that warm day, Schoenknecht offered something he called "brown skiing."

The Pinnacle ski trail at the top of Mohawk was covered with pine needles and hay atop a grassy base. To prepare skis, a slick mixture of kerosene and paraffin was applied with a paintbrush. About four hundred people showed up for the outing. Some dared to take a run on the pine needle–covered trail.

An October 22, 1950 article in *Hartford Courant Magazine* offered hope for the future when there was little natural snow. "Year 'Round Skiing for Connecticut" was the main headline. The subheadline read, "Artificial Clouds and Pine Needles Among Varied Plans of Walt Schoenknecht of Mohawk Mountain Ski Area in Cornwall."

The kerosene and wax mixture made the skiing especially fast. "It became increasingly slippery, and a straight schuss was the only way down," *Courant* ski writers Walter Pesko and Dorothy Nadler wrote. "Some of the better skiers were able to execute a christie at the bottom, while others simply fell to stop."

Schoenknecht also took a run on the slope. "He donned a pair of skis, went down in a hurry, and came up with the expression of delight that appears on all skier's faces after a good downhill run," the article reported. "Boy this is living," Schoenknecht said, brushing the straw from his trousers.

Before the 1950–51 ski season, Mohawk hosted the Connecticut Ski Council's outing in October. The Pinnacle ski trail was covered with pine needles. *Mohawk Mountain ski area.*

Bernice Boyd of the NAVA ski club called the day "wonderful, wonderful; all this beauty and we can ski, too."

Tony Gauba, of the Mountain Laurel Skiers, shouted as he whizzed down the mountain, "It's the best skiing I've seen this time of year."

Gus Sonne, another skier at the outing, said, "It's quite the stunt, and I'm surprised at the turnout."

Stunt or not, the *Courant* ski writers were impressed and optimistic about what the future could bring:

> *Mohawk Mountain with its pine needle skiing continues to prove itself to be a pioneer in the ski world. Last year, Walt Schoenknecht, manager, offered artificial snow made from ground up blocks of ice and sprayed it over the ground providing skiable snow. This resulted in a fast slope and was a great treat to snow hungry skiers.*
>
> *This year, Walt again is experimenting in the manufacture of his own clouds of mist, just above ground level, and seeding these clouds with crystals to produce falls of snow to the amount of a ton a minute. In the event that this is successful it would provide skiing throughout the season if Connecticut winters do not continue to climb in temperature and dwindle in snowfall.*

Schoenknecht told skiers at the outing that his "snow cloud" has not yet been successfully completed. The writers said that Walt "may be riding on a cloud, rather than making one." The article ended, "However with his past successful experiments, Walt may come up with the unexpected again."

Around the same time Schoenknecht was testing the snowmaking machine at Mohawk, he won a federal court case. Annalise Hartig of New York City sued him for $7,500, claiming that she had sustained a broken ankle after the ski tow suddenly stopped on January 17, 1948.

Skiers and tow operators had watched the case with particular interest, including the Connecticut Ski Council.

Before the jury deliberated the case, Judge Carroll C. Hincks told jurors that the issue was whether the sudden jerk of the rope tow had been caused by negligence of the operators. On December 14, 1950, it took the jury fifteen minutes to reject Hartig's claim for damages. For years, the case would be cited as a legal precedent in lawsuits filed against ski area operators.

WAYNE PIERCE APPLIES FOR
SNOWMAKING MACHINE PATENT

After the first snowmaking tests, on December 15, 1950, Wayne Pierce of the Tey Manufacturing Company applied for a U.S. patent on "the method for making snow and distributing snow."

Pierce wrote at the beginning of his application, "This invention relates to a new and useful method of making snow and to an installation for the economical manufacture and application of snow as a covering or coating on ski trails or the like in such quantities as to be useful for skiing and other winter sports. In recent years the enormous growth of interest in and the great increase in the number of people participating in winter sports has resulted in the growth or establishment of large-scale enterprises, the economic welfare of which is subject to the whims of the weather."

Pierce detailed the process of his invention with three sheets of numbered diagrams of the system and six pages of single-spaced descriptions of the parts and process of making snow.

On April 27, 1954, the patent—no. 2,676,471—was issued to "Wayne J. Pierce Jr., Milford, Connecticut, assignor to Tey Manufacturing Corporation." He was the first person to obtain a U.S. patent for the snowmaking system.

In 1956, Tey Manufacturing was sold to Emhart Corporation. The patent was kept by Emhart until 1959, when it was sold to Phil and Joe Tropeano's Larchmont company. The Tropeanos later sued other ski area operators for allegedly infringing on their snowmaking patent. The ski operators were successful in arguing that the process was discovered by Canadian engineers in the 1940s. The patent expired on April 27, 1971.

MASSACHUSETTS BROTHERS ENTER
SNOWMAKING BUSINESS

Brothers Phil and Joe Tropeano of Lexington, Massachusetts, became involved with Schoenknecht and Tey's snowmaking system in the fall of 1950. The Tropeanos started the Larchmont Farms and Irrigation Company in 1949. The company still manufactures and installs irrigation systems and is no longer in the snowmaking business.

"Early in 1950, the Tropeano brothers set out to develop a method of frost protection for citrus crops," according to a 1952 article in *American Ski Annual and Skiing Journal*. "The basic idea was to envelop an entire orchard in a cloud of warm, moisture-laden air by means of steam dispensed through special equipment. They encountered major and minor difficulties which they were still trying to iron out as of late December that year."

In December 1950, Larchmont wrote to Tey and suggested using its irrigation nozzle that protected crops from freezing. The Tropeanos said the nozzle could be modified to make snow.

"On December 13, Larchmont responded to Tey's request for a sample nozzle. These pieces of correspondence are important in that they indicate Walt Schoenknecht wasn't the only person who was forward thinking," wrote Nils Ericksen in a May 1980 article in *Ski Area Management*. "The Tropeano brothers persevered and never left the marketplace. Today, Larchmont Engineering has outlasted much of their original competition to be one of a handful of active snowmaking systems suppliers remaining in North America."

Because Larchmont was in the irrigation business, its experience was needed to supply piping and related equipment needed for Tey's snow machine.

The first tests in December 1950 uncovered some problems in the system. Phil Tropeano said in a December 11, 2008 *Boston Globe* interview, "We all went through a lot in the beginning. A lot of early problems with freezing nozzles and things like that. But [Tey] had their guns out first. We worked with them on the system. We cooperated with them instead of competing with each other."

Later, Larchmont realized the basic simplicity of producing some form of snow by mixing water and compressed air. It then undertook to sell complete snowmaking installations using a nozzle of its own design.

In the winter of 1950–51, Larchmont snowmaking systems were installed at Mount Sunapee State Park and at The Elms in Manchester, New Hampshire. The systems were cheaper and less elaborate than the Tey systems set up at Mohawk Mountain in Connecticut and Big Boulder in Pennsylvania.

"We figure a 24-nozzle unit—without an air compressor or water pump—would cost between $1,500 and $1,800," said Dave Heald, Sunapee's manager. "A compressor would be several thousand more, but we believe it is better to rent one by the hour. With 500 skiers on a weekday and 2,000 to 3,000 on Sundays, spending $4 to $6 each, the installation could be made to pay for itself."

April 27, 1954
W. M. PIERCE, JR
2,676,471

METHOD FOR MAKING AND DISTRIBUTING SNOW

Filed Dec. 14, 1950
3 Sheets—Sheet 1

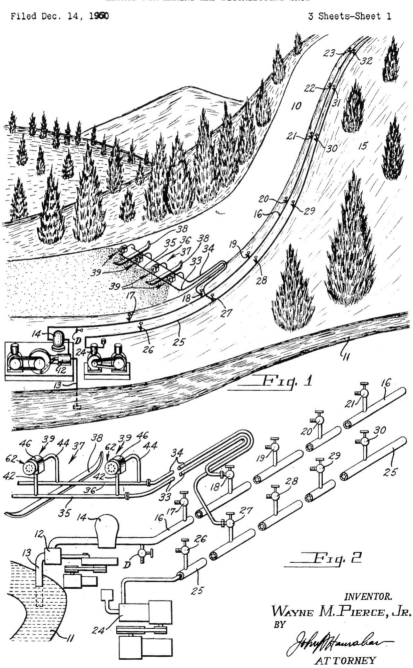

Fig. 1

Fig. 2

INVENTOR.
WAYNE M. PIERCE, JR.
BY

ATTORNEY

April 27, 1954   W. M. PIERCE, JR   2,676,471

METHOD FOR MAKING AND DISTRIBUTING SNOW

Filed Dec. 14, 1950   3 Sheets-Sheet 2

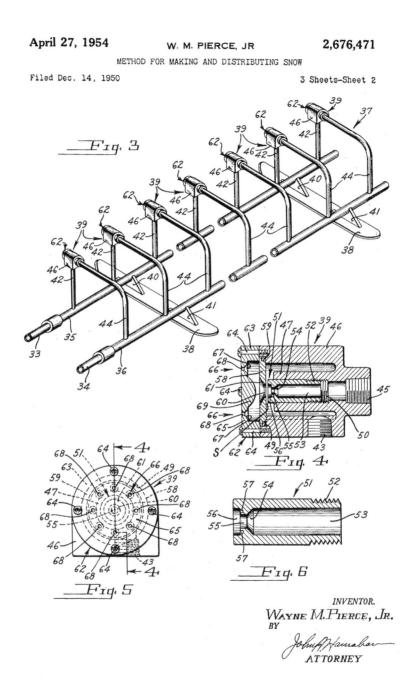

INVENTOR.
WAYNE M. PIERCE, JR.
BY
John Hanrahan
ATTORNEY

On December 15, 1950, Wayne Pierce of the Tey Manufacturing Company applied for a U.S. patent on "the method for making snow." He included these diagrams. *U.S. Patent Office.*

There was, however, the belief that the Tropeanos were violating the snowmaking patent granted to the Wayne Pierce and Tey engineers in 1954. In a January 10, 1957 memo, former Tey president Art Hunt wrote to J.R. Hobson, a lawyer and Emhart Corporation secretary. Hobson was responsible for protecting Emhart's patents and trademarks, according to his May 19, 1994 obituary in the *Hartford Courant*):

> *Larchmont Farms and the Tropeano brothers were engaged by Walter Schoenknecht of Mohawk Mountain Ski area to furnish the irrigation pipes, valves, etc. during the early fall 1950. Mr. J.C. Tropeano visited our offices on December 1, 1950 and expressed his desire to work with us on the installation of the snowmaking equipment.*
>
> *We attempted to caution him of the many unknown features of this system that could possibly cause problems. However, he chose to disregard us on approximately the same date that we filed for a patent* [December 15, 1950]. *His apparent reason that on that date he discovered that his irrigation nozzle if fed compressed air and water would produce snow. A Boston paper write-up published on approximately that date states that he inadvertently left a nozzle running all night and to his surprise found snow in the morning.*
>
> *His early years resulted in adverse relations with ski areas because of his foolish guarantees which after installing equipment were never able to be fulfilled. His new nozzle, still an internal mix and being used at Bousquet's* [ski area in Pittsfield, Massachusetts] *has an electric heating element in it. There is no question he is exploiting our patent.*

1950–51: FIRST SNOWMAKING SYSTEM
INSTALLED AT MOHAWK

A United Press article featured the headlines "341 N.E. Ski Resorts Confident of Prosperous '50–51 Season" and "Good Supply of Snow Expected, If Not Natural Then by Using New Snow-Making Machine."

In the 1950–51 season, Tey installed the first snowmaking system at Mohawk Mountain and then at Split Rock Lodge (now Big Boulder) in Pennsylvania's Pocono Mountains.

Robert Vine, president of Lehigh Coal and Navigation, which owned the Split Rock Lodge, was optimistic of the snow machine's future. "We believe

From left to right: Mohawk Mountain manager Walt Schoenknecht, Tey engineers David Richey and Arthur Hunt test a snowmaking machine at the Mohawk ski area in 1950. *Mohawk Mountain ski area.*

we are immune to the tricks of the weather," he told the Shenandoah, Pennsylvania *Evening Herald*. "The beauty of this process is the fact that the snow quality may vary from dry powder to nearly wet snow, including the granular or 'corn' snow being sought by skiers as the best."

The news article reported on Monday, December 18, 1950, "Experiments on the revolutionary process began today for the manufacture of snow at the famous ski slope at nearby Split Rock Lodge in the Pocono Mountains."

On December 10, 1950, in the *Bridgeport (CT) Sunday Herald*, an article was headlined, "Bright Hope for Ski Fans...Mohawk Trail to Use Artificial Snow Whenever Nature Fails":

> *Mark Twain, who lived for many years in Connecticut, is credited with the statement "Everybody talks about the weather, but no one ever does anything about it." Another New England allusion to its weather is to the effect that if you don't like it now, wait a few minutes and it will change.*
>
> *Chief weather bugaboo to Connecticut ski slope operators as well as those farther north is the uncertainty of snow. This has been particularly noticeable during the past few winters, but at least one Connecticut man is out to beat the elements this year.*

Walter Schoenknecht was granted permission three years ago by the Connecticut Park and Forest Department to develop a skiing area on Mohawk Mountain in Cornwall. The first winter found nature very co-operative and Connecticut skiers had good snow cover on many weekends when it was poor to the north. Then two warmer winters resulted in spotty snow conditions.

Mohawk was an easy choice for the first snowmaking system. The Tey engineers had skied at Mohawk; it was about a ninety-minute drive from their homes in southern Connecticut and had a good water supply. And there was also Walt Schoenknecht, an enthusiastic cheerleader of their efforts.

In a December 15, 1950 *Hartford Courant* article, Schoenknecht said that his snowmaking machine was still in the experimental stage. He said all the necessary pipes and equipment had been assembled so that the moment the temperature gets low enough, Mohawk will be ready to test the system.

"If this proves successful," the *Courant* article read, "skiers will be in the position to ski every week on smooth, well planned and manicured trails covered with man-made snow providing spring-like temperatures do not prevail. Only a blizzard like that of '47 could be better news."

On Wednesday, December 27, 1950, Schoenknecht told the *Courant*, "Ski conditions will be good through the weekend and that, if necessary, the area's new snow-making machine will be used to recondition spots that show signs of wearing out."

Schoenknecht told the *New York Times* that the system included 1,600 feet of aluminum pipe, two pumps and a compressor. A pond at the bottom of Mohawk supplied the water. "We waited until it got cold enough and started the compressor at 3 o'clock in the morning," he said. "Sure enough, huge masses of snow began to pour out, but the nozzle emitted a tremendous shrieking sound that could be heard from miles around. The Cornwall Fire Department came racing up, thinking maybe, the heating system in the lodge blew up." Two weeks later, adjustments to the nozzle eliminated the shrieking sound while producing snow. However, according to

The original Tey nozzle had one central water jet and two air jets. In the mid-1950s, Tey became a division of Skyworker, with the manufacturer's name seen on the nozzle. *New England Ski Museum.*

the Cornwall Historical Society, "This time it emitted an ultrasonic whistle that made all the dogs in the area bark; more adjustments were made."

Developing a successful snowmaking system took years. The first tests found many kinks in the system— water lines froze or broke, compressors blew out and the sprayer nozzles balked. Work crews put in long nights repairing the breakdowns. Adjustments to the snowmaking system required re-engineered air compressors, special metal piping and water pumps to produce better results.

During the crucial testing period of the snowmaking machine in the 1950–51 season, Schoenknecht gave newspapers updated information on the progress of the device. His intense promotion and devotion to the machine led some newspapers, like the *Boston Globe*, to call Schoenknecht the "inventor of snowmaking."

A December 29, 1950 Associated Press article stated, "Ski slope operators still don't know if they have a device on their hands that can revolutionize the winter sports business after testing a new snowmaker here last night. A trial of the new type of snow machine at the Mohawk Mountain ski area ended inconclusively when below zero cold froze feed lines of the device after only a small amount of snow was produced. Walter Schoenknecht, manager of the state forest and Arthur Hunt, president of the Tey Manufacturing Co., inventor of the snow-making process, said another test would be attempted under more favorable water conditions."

BIG BREAKTHROUGH COMES AFTER NEW YEAR'S DAY

Finally, success! "The Mohawk ski area is set to thumb its nose at New England's temperamental weatherman," *Eastern Skier* magazine reported in its January 15, 1951 issue. "Walter R. Schoenknecht, manager of the state forest area, announces the end of a long testing period for the snowmaker developed by the Tey Mfg. Co. of Milford, CT. Successful experiments carried out over the long New Year weekend added almost three inches of man-made snow to an eight-inch packed base. Schoenknecht now plans to use the snowmaker every night over weekends to assure improved skiing for the next day. Similar tests, on a smaller scale, are being carried out at the Split Rock ski area in White Haven, Pa."

Mohawk's $25,000 snowmaking system was crisscrossed with two miles of four-inch aluminum pipe and a mile of green plastic hoses in varying

Walter Schoenknecht
Mohawk Ski Area
Corwall, Conn.

JANUARY 15, 1951

EASTERN SKIER

VOL. III   NO. 6   Entered as Second Class Matter at the Post Office at Boston, Mass.   BOSTON, MASS. $1 a year — 10 issues   TEN CENTS

SNOW MAKING IS 'PRACTICAL'

$25,000 Air-Water Sprayer Network Operates Successfully at Mohawk

By FLORENCE ZUCKERBRAUN
Eastern SKIER Correspondent

CORNWALL, Conn.—The Mohawk ski area is set to thumb its nose at New England's temperamental weatherman.

Walter R. Schoenknecht, manager of the state forest area announces the end of a long testing period for the snowmaker developed by the Tey Mfg. Co. of Milford, Conn.

9 College Teams Enter Dartmouth's Four-Event Meet

HANOVER, N.H. — Nine college ski-team racers and jumpers will fight for the Dartmouth Carnival Cup in the Big Green's 36th annual Invitational Intercollegiate four-event tournament here Feb. 10-11.

Entries have been received from Denver University, M.I.T., McGill, Middlebury, Syracuse, and the state universities of Maine, New Hampshire and Vermont.

Cross-country and slalom events will be held Feb. 9; downhill and jumping will be held the next day.

Construction of the traditional snow

The machine, he says, has a definite practical application for manufacturement natural fall. Successful experiments carried out over the long New Year weekend added almost three inches of man-made snow to a eight-inch packed base over a large slope and trail section.

Schoenknecht now plans to use the snow-maker every night over week ends to assure improved skiing for the next day.

The machine, which works on the principle of a giant atomizer, mixes air and water under heavy pressure forming a vapor cloud seeded to crystalize as snow.

$25,000 INSTALLATION
Mohawk's nine-tow area is criss-crossed with two miles of four-inc

'MOHAWK SNOW-JOB — In large photo, left to right, Area Mgr. Walt Schosnknecht and Engineers David Richey and Arthur Hunt, who developed the system, check one of the 'atomizers' which produced snow at Mohawk ski area. In insert photo, Eastern SKIER'S Flo Zuckerbraun (left) and skier Lorraine Mercier of Waterbury, Conn. study fir tree frosted by the man-made snow.

The news of the successful test of the snowmaking machine at Mohawk Mountain was on the front page of *Eastern Skier* on January 15, 1951. Note Walt Schoenknecht's address in the upper left. *New England Ski Museum.*

diameters. "The machine, which works on the principle of a giant atomizer, mixes air and water under heavy pressure, forming a vapor cloud seeded to crystalize as snow," according to the *Eastern Skier* article.

Ski writer Henry Mooberry Jr. of the *Herald News* of Passaic, New Jersey, traveled to Mohawk to check out the snow conditions. "While skiing at Cornwall last weekend this writer noticed that the slope with the man-made snow lacked the barren spots of the natural covered slopes and was much faster running. The only discrepancy in the slope was the wet iced spots which slowed the skier considerably," Mooberry wrote in his January 5, 1951 column. "This machine might well be the boon that many of the money-losing areas of the east are looking for if conditions continue as they have during the last two seasons."

Schoenknecht was becoming a master at spreading news about Mohawk Mountain's successful use of a snowmaking machine.

After the *Kukla, Fran and Ollie* show on December 26, 1951, Schoenknecht entered into a new medium, appearing on television. On the *Connecticut Spotlight* program on WNHC-TV, now WTNH, he showed slides and spoke about the improvements at Mohawk Mountain that season. This was at a time when radio was still the main source of news and entertainment. The *Hartford Courant*'s listings of programs on the day of Schoenknecht's TV appearance included 276 radio shows and only 33 television programs. Popular TV shows included *Howdy Doody* and *Tom Corbett, Space Cadet*.

SNOWMAKING BEGINS TO EXPAND TO OTHER SKI AREAS

In 1952, Tey installed the first major commercial snowmaking installation at Grossinger's resort in New York's Catskill Mountains. The resort's management said that machine-made snow "is no longer a luxury, but an absolute necessity for our winter operation."

Over the next decades, advances in snowmaking technology would continue. In 1958, Alden Hanson filed a patent for a new type of snowmaking machine that had a fan inside it. In 1961, he was awarded the patent for the use of the fan, particulate water and the optional use of a nucleating agent (dirt particles). It would take a quarter century for the snow fan to become the most common type of snowmaker.

In 1952, Tey installed the first major commercial snowmaking system at Grossinger's resort in New York's Catskill Mountains. *New England Ski Museum.*

Mohawk used this type of snow gun in the 1970s. Hoses, similar to fire hoses, were used to carry water to the snowmaking gun. *Mohawk Mountain ski area.*

In 1969, three engineers at Columbia University's Lamont Labs received a patent for a rotating fan blade that atomized water in the front, which froze and became snow. Today, Mohawk uses snow fans to cover most of its terrain with snow. *Mohawk Mountain ski area.*

THE BIRTH OF SNOWMAKING

Unlike the earlier Tey snowmaker, Hanson's device produced more snow more quickly, used less energy and was much quieter. Hanson's invention is considered the pioneer patent for all fan snowmaking machines.

In 1969, three engineers at Columbia University's Lamont Labs received a patent for "a rotating fan blade that was impacted with water from the rear, resulting in mechanically atomized water leaving the front which froze and became snow," according to theinventors.org. Today, fan-type snowmaking machines are found at most ski areas, including Mohawk Mountain.

Snow Making International (SMI) is a world leader in snowmaking systems. Many of its systems are automated to produce snow when weather conditions are good for snowmaking.

In 1964, there were 140 ski areas in the eastern United States and Canada that had some type of snowmaking systems. In 2023, the National Ski Areas Association said that roughly 87 percent of 337 ski resorts the trade group represents have snowmaking capabilities.

TEY ENGINEERS MADE LITTLE MONEY OFF SNOW MACHINE

Art Hunt, former Tey president, wrote in a 1990 *Ski Area Management* article that even with first snowmaking installations working at Mohawk and Big Boulder in Pennsylvania, "we could see the equipment needed to coat ski slopes would have to be tremendous in size and extremely costly and sold the company and patents to Emhart Corporation in 1956."

Hunt added, "Over the past years, the Tey group realized no remuneration from the snowmaking invention, but we have had the satisfaction of knowing that our development altered and improved the skiing surface. I still ski and I'm glad the machine snow is there."

Tey was more successful in manufacturing Skyworkers, self-powered aerial-lift machine bucket trucks used by power companies, telephone linemen and tree surgeons. The Skyworker Corporation was created in a merger of Tey Manufacturing and Maxwell Equipment Corporation. The first Skyworkers were mounted on trucks, trailers and dollies or tractors; had either one or two insulated "crow's nests" of fiberglass; and used many hydraulic principles. By 1951, its products were being used by more than forty utility companies.

The *Hartford Courant* reported on August 17, 1956, that Emhart paid Skyworker more than $600,000 to acquire the Milford, Connecticut company.

David Richey, one of Tey's partners, "was a key player in the design of the first aerial lift-machine that is used exclusively by the telephone and electric industry, a product he stayed involved with for 40 years," according to his obituary.

Most of the Tey founders remained in Connecticut years after their snowmaking invention—Wayne Pierce in Orange, Art Hunt in Milford and Richey in Woodbridge from 1954 to 1998.

Of the three Tey company founders, Richey was the oldest but the last to die. Wayne Pierce, born in Clinton, Massachusetts, died on May 7, 1985, at age sixty-nine. Arthur R. Hunt, born in the Naugatuck Valley town of Ansonia, Connecticut, died on March 30, 1993, at age seventy-eight. Richey, born in Dover, Ohio, died on March 28, 2003, at age ninety-two.

A January 31, 1957 article in the *Bridgeport Post* announced Wayne Pierce's appointment as vice-president of engineering and manufacturing for Norden-Ketay Corporation in Norwalk and Stamford, Connecticut. Pierce's development of a snowmaking machine was not forgotten. "Active in research and development with Tey, Mr. Pierce designed and developed an artificial snow machine which is used extensively today at ski resorts throughout the United States," the article stated.

MOHAWK FOUNDER OPENS MOUNT SNOW IN VERMONT

One year before he opened the Mohawk ski area in Connecticut, Walt Schoenknecht discovered a mountain in southern Vermont that would later become the Mount Snow ski resort.

For years, Schoenknecht had been chasing a dream of creating a ski resort that would become like no other. The big difference was that it would cater to novices and intermediate skiers who wanted to enjoy the day both on and off the slopes. Radical new ski lifts, designed by Schoenknecht, would carry more skiers to the top of the mountain and enclose them in weather-protected gondolas. His other innovations included wider, easy-to-ski trails and off-slope activities, including an outdoor heated swimming pool and a lively après ski scene. All were introduced during a time when skiing was exploding, bringing thousands of younger, less experienced skiers and new families to the slopes.

There were also affordable ski weeks that included lift tickets, lessons, a place to sleep and an opportunity to mingle—and maybe find some romance with other like-minded skiers.

Schoenknecht had a wish list for finding the right mountain: it had to be accessible from main roads, have a long ski season, include several peaks and be close to major population centers in the Northeast. Sounded like a tall order, but Walt Schoenknecht, a flatlander from Connecticut's shoreline, found it in the tiny and nearly deserted town of West Dover, Vermont.

It happened on October 2, 1946, at the peak of a 3,600-foot snow-covered mountain. "I stood at the top of that mountain—Mount Pisgah

Walt Schoenknecht stands with a Mount Snow sign shortly after the Vermont ski area opened in December 1954. *Mohawk Mountain ski area.*

they called her then—and I looked all around me," Schoenknecht recalled in an October 1961 *Sports Illustrated* article titled "Vermont's Phenomenal Snowman."

He said, "I looked down at the snow at my feet; October snow, eighteen inches deep. I looked out at that broad and beautiful valley falling away below me. And most of all, I looked far off into the future. And there, just waiting for me, I saw the ski resort of my dreams. It would be the largest in the world, it would be second to none, it would be fabulous."

Years after Schoenknecht opened Mohawk, he took a crucial step in opening the ski resort of his dreams. "One day in 1953," according to the *Sports Illustrated* article, "Schoenknecht drove again to Mt. Pisgah, took another admiring turn around the grounds and presented himself at the front door of the owner's farmhouse. Schoenknecht outlined his proposal briefly and the price agreed upon for 500 acres was $15,000. In those days, the land was so little regarded that the tax assessor's appraisal was a mere $1,500."

Schoenknecht would later name the mountain after a fifth-generation farmer and cattleman who owned the land. The farmer's name was Reuben—Reuben Snow. A perfect name for Walt's ski resort of his dreams.

Schoenknecht would later obtain a lease from the U.S. Forest Service for ski trails of the upper portion of Mount Snow. "He went to Vermont with his father, and he called back very excited that he found the place. And I said where is it? And he said in West Dover in Vermont," his wife, Peg, recalled in the 1994 PBS documentary *Mount Snow—The First Forty Years*. "He just had a feeling for the terrain and that this would be good; and we need an upsweep this way and a little curve here. And he cut it that way and then graded it," Peg said. "He stood out there and told the guys what he wanted, the bulldozer operators. He knew exactly how to do it."

After he bought the land for the ski area, Schoenknecht sought financial backers for the ambitious development. Holders of a $1,000 share in the Mount Snow Development Corporation got free use of the lifts for a ten-year period.

Many of those stockholders had skied at Mohawk Mountain in Connecticut. Many had hocked everything, except their skis, to raise the $1,000. One of the big investors was twenty-six-year-old Winston Lauder of New Haven, vice-president of the development company, who took one look at Mount Snow and said, "This is it."

On December 4, 1953, West Dover residents read in the *Brattleboro Daily Reformer* that a $3 million ski area was planned in their backyard, just off Handle Road. "The Mt. Snow Ski Development Corporation, headed by Walter R. Schoenknecht of East Haven, Connecticut had purchased the Reuben Snow farm as the start of the project, which would subsequently include trails and lifts to the crest of Mt. Pisgah, and even a heated outdoor swimming pool for winter use," according to the *History of Dover* book. "Dover's only real industry, besides farming, was to begin. In the ski news of the city newspapers, the development was called Mount Snow, and this is the name by which it will be generally known."

One day earlier, Connecticut residents got the first word of the Mount Snow development from Walt Pesko and Artie Donovan's ski column in one of those "city newspapers," the *Hartford Courant*. It wasn't front-page news; it was buried halfway down the column with a small headline of "Schoenknecht Duet."

It read, "Plans are in the making for Walt Schoenknecht to expand his skiing empire. 'The mountain has fantastic possibilities,' he said. Walt assures us that he will still be with Mohawk Mountain and the new area is a supplement to the old. It is located halfway between Brattleboro and Bennington, north of Wilmington, just off Vermont's scenic Molly Stark Drive. Wilmington is ideally adapted for winter use, with adequate accommodations."

The columnists continued, "The new area will take several years to develop and cost between two and three million dollars. Construction will start in the spring. No opening date has been announced, of course. Oh, what a dream! But we know Walt will turn this into reality. He has the needed enthusiasm and can depend on the wholehearted support of Connecticut skiers."

VERMONT BEFORE MOUNT SNOW

Before Mount Snow opened, Vermont experienced years of declining population, an increasing number of abandoned farms and less manufacturing. "Many young people also listened to the call of the West with its fertile fields and the promise of adventure, or of the city with anticipated proper wages and bright lights," according to a Dover history book published in 1961. "Without youth strength to help keep the farm going, many owners, usually the older ones, moved to a village or town, for easier living."

Looking for ways to bring more people to the Green Mountain State, the Vermont Board of Agriculture in 1892 published a pamphlet describing the state's resources and the many homes and farms for sale. One of those farms up for sale was in West Dover, Vermont. "Village farm for sale at a bargain to close out an estate," the pamphlet advertised. "Situated in West Dover, Vt. A neat and pleasant village on the branch of the Deerfield River. Good school, church and two stores. Only six miles from the railroad at Wilmington, over one of the best roads in the state. The farm contains 87 acres or more; 32 in the village."

The farm also had a "good" one-and-a-half-story house, three barns and "never failing water in house and barn." The asking price? "All was $2,000." The pamphlet also mentioned Vermont as a destination for a summer retreat with mountain views, many lakes, streams and scenic valleys. "It has not until recently been known that Vermont offers more beautiful and restful retreats for those who seek a refuge from the summer heat and dust of the cities than does any other part of New England."

The pamphlet may have caught the attention of President Theodore Roosevelt's son, who in the early 1900s purchased a home with his wife in West Dover. The building at Two Tannery Road is now a restaurant. "According to local residents with keen memories and to TR's granddaughter, President Roosevelt was known to come here for a retreat," according to the restaurant's website. "Often arriving unannounced at the old railway station [in Wilmington], he would be given a ride by one of the local residents."

By the 1920s, Dover had several farmhouses open for summer guests. In the fall, the homes welcomed deer hunters. Some of those guests would later purchase summer homes on Handle Road, near the future site of Mount Snow.

"The town's meadows were never decorated with blaring signboards, its villages dotted with overnight guest signs. Nor its roads accented with gift shops or hot dog stands," according to the Dover history book. "The town's roads have been too remote from main summer-traveled highways' most cars sped through Dover to reach towns advertising hotels."

According to the Dover Historical Society, by the late 1940s, the town's population had shrunk to the lowest number since 1790. "There were no paved roads. The telephone call from East Dover to West Dover was long distance. All telephone lines were crank phones and everyone was on eight party-lines. During storms, it was not unusual for electricity to be out for three to four days. The winter road crew consisted of three married men and selectmen were also expected to plow roads. Today's Route 100, then numbered Route 8, was dirt in the summer and mud in the spring."

SNEAK PREVIEW OF MOUNT SNOW

Two months before Mount Snow opened, the *Berkshire Eagle* gave an expansive look at Vermont's newest ski area. Headlines above the article read, "New Mount Snow Ski Area to Have Two Chairlifts Running This Winter" and "Promoter Walt Schoenknecht Plans Gigantic Development. Seven Miles of Uphill Lifts Anticipated Within a Period of Five to Seven Years—Huge Canteen, Outdoor Pool to Be Built."

The *Eagle* sent two sportswriters, John Vander Voort and John Hitchcock, to get a sneak preview of "New England's newest and most ambitious ski development," the October 13, 1954 article stated. There were also two photos of a glass-walled sundeck and another of Schoenknecht and Vander Voort at the new "monorail chairlift."

Under the small headline "Stake in the Future," the article began, "Three miles outside this isolated village [of West Dover, Vermont] on a 3,600-foot mountain already inscribed with a network of wide, contoured trails, Schoenknecht is gambling on his future on a mammoth four-million-dollar winter sports project that will rival Stowe [in Vermont] and Sun Valley [in Idaho]. For skiers this season, one 2,000-foot double chair lift is already operating, and another 3,700-footer will be ready for the opening. They will service five trails and two slopes. But it doesn't stop there. Within five to seven years, Schoenknecht plans to have seven miles of chairlifts connecting a pattern of trails for skiers of all ability."

OPENING DAY AT MOUNT SNOW

Before Mount Snow opened on December 12, 1954, existing ski areas built in the 1930s and 1940s had mostly steep, twisting, ungroomed trails and bare-bones amenities. Some ski "lodges" were converted huts and shelters warmed by potbelly stoves. And restrooms were outhouses.

In his 1984 *Great North American Ski Book*, author I. William Berry labeled this mid-1950s and early '60s period the "Golden Age" of skiing. It was a time that began to focus on the pampering of the novice and intermediate skier—a path first blazed by Schoenknecht.

"Mount Snow and Schoenknecht," Berry wrote, "proved that the atmosphere and terrain that Stowe (and the smaller Mad River Glen) in Vermont were self-limiting and that most Americans would not tolerate the (expressed or implied) arrogance that went along with that pioneer (ski) period. Only the expert would be allowed to enjoy skiing."

Berry wrote that Schoenknecht felt everybody should enjoy themselves as much on the first day on skis as they would later as experts. "He also realized that skiers—especially the novice and intermediate—do not live by skiing alone," Berry wrote. "Nor do they want to be intimidated and scorned by the more competent. Rather, they want to be welcomed and entertained and coddled, and since they're paying money, they should get what they want."

John Fry, longtime editor of *SKI Magazine* and author of *The Story of Modern Skiing*, wrote that Schoenknecht's "widening of trails was ahead of its time in the 1950s and was quickly copied by other area operators, who admired his creativity."

Win Lauder, a former vice-president of Mount Snow, said in a 1974 *Hartford Courant* ski column by Pinky Stein, "Walt set the pattern and wrote the blueprint for ski areas old and new since 1954. Prewar and post-war ski areas were created by rich nuts who wanted their own ice cream cones."

An aerial view of Mount Snow in the early 1960s. Note the absence of development in the lower portion of the photo. *Mohawk Mountain ski area.*

Lauder said that Schoenknecht brought about a reformation of the ski industry and made skiing available to everyone on a scale never known. "The super-large base lodge was his baby. So was the very wide ski trail and the following of the fall line in the laying out of trails."

Lauder said that Schoenknecht also "created social change in convincing by example the U.S. Forest Service, the Green Mountain Power Company, the New England Telephone Company and the Vermont Assembly and Senate that Vermont mountain development would revitalize the decaying heartland of the state. Walt received the ultimate compliment from a Vermont banker who told him that in an era in southern Vermont when everyone owned the storekeeper…you brought life to this valley where there was death."

A September 6, 1961 article in the *Rutland Herald* stated, "Walt Schoenknecht inaugurated the shift to off-the-ground transportation when he opened Mount Snow at West Dover in December 1954. The resort, adding lifts and improvements of every kind each season, grew and grew, until the directors were able to announce last year that Mount Snow was the largest ski resort in the world. That fall, its many chairlifts sprawled over the mountain like a giant cobweb, officials listed an hourly uphill capacity of 11,000."

Lew Cuyler, a writer with the *North Adams Transcript*, said that in the early days of Mount Snow, "Walt was everywhere. You'd see him skiing the trails and later striding through the base lodge, a tall rangy man with close cropped hair who moved with the quickness and the grace of a cat."

THINGS THAT MADE MOUNT SNOW DIFFERENT

Apart from the wide ski trails and ego-boosting terrain for novices and intermediate skiers, Mount Snow had some revolutionary and unusual attractions not seen at other ski areas at the time, including the following.

THE "AIR CAR." The aerial tramway cars looked like something from *The Jetsons*, the futuristic 1960s cartoon TV show. Installed in the 1964–65 season, the aerial tramway ran two thousand feet between the Snow Lake Lodge and the base area. It was removed in 1977 after Mount Snow, hemorrhaging from financial debt, was sold to Killington's Sherburne Corporation for $4.5 million.

TWO HIGH-CAPACITY "MONORAIL LIFTS." Debuted in Mount Snow's first season, the lifts, designed by Schoenknecht, were built by the Link Belt Company of New York. They consisted almost entirely of welded, four-inch I-beams. The chairs glided up steel rails on double rollers, pulled by sturdy link belts. Short towers were fifteen feet apart, and the seats, forty feet apart, moved close to the ground. Each of the lifts had an unheard-of capacity of 1,180 riders per hour—double that of conventional cable chairs. There was, however, one problem: droplets of grease fell on skiers riding the lifts. The next year, Schoenknecht had shields installed above the chairlift seats.

KEEP YOUR SKIS ON GONDOLAS. The idea came from Schoenknecht's back problems and his reluctance to take off his skis for every ride. The two gondolas built by the Italian Charlevaro & Sabio Company also had a bubble design that protected skies from wind and cold. One of the two-person gondolas went to the summit and the other three-quarters the way up the mountain. The first gondola started running in 1965 and the second in 1969. The last bubble gondola was removed in 1986 after some gondolas fell off the cable to the ground.

Top: The chairlift on the right was a monorail lift designed by Walt Schoenknecht. There was one problem with the lift: grease fell on skiers riding the chairlift. *Author's collection.*

Bottom: Two gondolas built by the Italian Charlevaro & Sabio Company had a bubble design that protected skiers from wind and cold. *Author's collection.*

"FOUNTAIN MOUNTAIN." In 1968, Schoenknecht added something new that would extend Mount Snow's ski season. The fountain, which threw ten thousand gallons of water in the air in a man-made lake, would run all winter long. "This year we are really going for Fountain Mountain that will be over 200 feet high and skiable as corn snow in May and June, with a portable ski-tow right up to its peak," Schoenknecht told *the Brattleboro Reformer*. "Thousands and thousands of tons of ice will come from that fountain spray this winter, and people will come from miles around to see it, and to ski it—in June."

His daughter, Carol Lugar, recalled in a 1994 PBS documentary, "The first year [the fountain] wasn't all that big, but then it got to be a game to see how big it could get. And it did get to an enormous proportion. It was a great place to fool around in the spring with sleds and skis. There were races on it and it was a trademark of Snow Lake Lodge as well to see how much ice you can have on your windshield in the parking lot."

A HEATED OUTDOOR SWIMMING POOL. Debuted during the 1958–59 season, the pool, heated to ninety-six degrees, was surrounded by glass panels to protect swimmers from chilly winds. The pool featured diving boards and lounge chairs around the pool. The pool was a focal point in ski movies and magazine articles on Mount Snow's unusual attractions.

THE FARMER AND THE FROGS. Schoenknecht named a tavern on the fourth floor of the main base lodge after Reuben Snow, the farmer who owned the land before Mount Snow. The *Greenfield Recorder* reported on March 15, 1969, the tavern had a new sound: the deep-throated croaking of frogs. "President Walt Schoenknecht and founder of Mount Snow had a total of 20 frogs put in the tropical garden—14 small bullfrogs and six larger ones—to give it a more authentic air. They were placed in the ponds that are part of the lush tropical garden in the restaurant which overlooks the slopes."

CLASSIC ALPINE SKI LODGES. In 1956, a summit lodge with an observation deck opened. An additional base lodge with a classic alpine style opened during the 1960–61 season. The design of the lodge would later be used in the construction of Mohawk's new lodge in 1964, The Sundance area also had traditional chairlifts designed by Charlevaro & Sabio that ended the dripping grease problems from the chain link chairs.

Just before the Christmas/New Year's week in 1954, the weather played tricks with New England skiing, improving conditions at some, while spoiling it at others.

"Big Bromley at Manchester, Vermont, victim of sudden warmth and heavy rain, suffered attendance pangs as many skiers headed home early,

A lodge was built on the summit of Mount Snow in 1956. An early morning fire on January 19, 1969, destroyed the building. Clouds prevented people from seeing the fire. *Author's collection.*

convinced they couldn't handle the boiler plate ice that crusted slopes and trails," the *Berkshire Eagle* reported on December 20, 1954. "An iron-like crust made skiing almost impossible."

Dedication of a new 6,200-foot double chair lift at Stowe's Spruce Peak had to be delayed because of gale-force winds.

At Mount Snow, "despite a two-inch rainfall Saturday, there was from six to 36 inches of snow on the mountain, topped by a breakable crust. It snowed lightly all day. There were a few icy spots, but no bare areas and skiing was good. Full day tickets for all the lifts were $4," according to the *Berkshire Eagle* article.

On December 16, 1954, the *Bennington Evening Banner* ran a photo of Schoenknecht and Carol standing in front of the Mount Snow lodge's stone fireplace. Also pictured were Orla Larsen, manager, and carpenter Percy Haskins. The caption read, "Schoenknecht and Larsen anticipate a fair weekend of sliding at the new resort despite rain and warm weather this week. They said that all facilities are expected to be usable, even though the ski area will operate on a 'test' basis only and the management 'guarantees nothing.'"

Mount Snow would end up having a snowy first season. Two blizzards in late March and early April 1955 extended the season well into spring.

POOR ROADS IN MOUNT SNOW'S EARLY DAYS

Schoenknecht's opening of Mount Snow came at an opportune time: the beginning of the interstate highway system, which created limited-access highways, allowing faster speeds with no traffic lights.

It began when President Dwight D. Eisenhower signed legislation on January 26, 1956. It included $50 billion to build a U.S. interstate highway system over a ten-year period. Eisenhower, who served as the supreme commander of the Allied forces in World War II, saw the need for an efficient and high-speed highway network.

According to the U.S. Army, Eisenhower was an observer in the first Transcontinental Motor Company in 1919. The operation was a kind of road test for military vehicles to identify the challenges of moving troops from coast to coast on existing infrastructure. The road trip covered more than three thousand miles from Washington, D.C., to San Francisco. It included seventy-nine vehicles of all sizes and nearly three hundred soldiers.

Eisenhower found that the existing highway system was inadequate with its patchwork of paved and unpaved roads, bridges too low to pass under and different grades of roads. After World War II, Eisenhower wrote in his presidential memoirs that he had seen "the superlative system of German autobahn—[the] national highways crossing that country." He wrote the advanced European highway system helped resupply the Allied forces across France and into Germany.

Eisenhower's plan to construct a vast system of interconnected highways was based on four points, according to the U.S. Army:

- Safety. The plan cited thirty-six thousand traffic fatalities annually and the multi-billion-dollar effect on the economy.
- Road conditions. The physical effect of existing roads and the effect on vehicle ownership. Poorly maintained roads adversely affected the economy by increasing transportation costs.
- National security. In the late 1950s Cold War era with the Soviet Union there was the threat to national security. The pervasive threat of nuclear attack on the United States called for the ability to execute the emergency evacuation of large cities and the quick movement of troops essential to national defense.
- U.S. economy. Improvements in transportation must keep up with the growing population. Road improvement was seen as an essential use of taxpayer money. The committee that

The first section of I-91 in Vermont opened from the Massachusetts border to Exit 1 in Brattleboro on November 1, 1958. *Federal Highway Administration.*

prepared the report was headed by General Lucius Clay, an aide to Eisenhower in the war and after "Ike" was elected president in 1952. Clay's committee said the interstate highway system would improve the well-being of the economy through "speedy, safe transcontinental travel" that could improve "farm to market movement."

Not mentioned was how it would improve the ski industry. It would take a few years before interstate highways would provide faster access and easy driving to Mount Snow and other ski areas.

The first portion of Interstate 91 opened on November 1, 1958, from the Massachusetts border to Exit 1 in Brattleboro after two years of construction. In Massachusetts, by 1960, a few miles of I-91 had been built starting from the Connecticut and Vermont state lines. Connecticut's first construction of an interstate began in 1958 in the southwest part of the state. It would take until 1970 for all segments of I-91 to be completed from Connecticut to Vermont.

A 1954 highway map by the Vermont Department of Highways included a brief section on winter sports, noting there are about thirty-five winter sports centers. "The best snow conditions in the East are found along the Green Mountain chain. At the highest elevations the annual average snowfall is about 120 inches and the best spots last from mid-December into April."

The map noted Vermont's main and connecting highways are kept well plowed and sanded throughout the winter. "This is primarily for the practical reason that vast quantities of milk must get to markets in metropolitan areas and secondly, so that motorists can get around. This is all the good in the minds of recreational bound skiers, thousands in number who drive to popular skiing areas."

In the 1954–55 ski season, the most direct and mostly paved north/south highway routes to Mount Snow were Routes 7 and 5. From the east and west, Route 9 (the Molly Stark Trail) follows the same path it does today, from Brattleboro to Wilmington to Bennington. From Boston, motorists traveled on Route 2 to Shelburne Falls, Massachusetts, and then took Routes 112 and 8 to Wilmington. Once in Wilmington, drivers took Route 8 (now Route 100). The road was paved until the intersection with Handle Road.

In 1954, Route 100, now known as the "Skiers' Highway," was farther north of Mount Snow, running between Weston and Newport. Today, after road improvements in the 1960s and the renumbering of roads, Route 100 runs more than two hundred miles in Vermont. Ski areas on or near Route 100 include Mount Snow, Okemo, Killington, Sugarbush, Mad River Glen and Stowe.

Driving the last few miles on the gravel road to Mount Snow sometimes proved difficult for drivers. The *Brattleboro Reformer* ran a front-page story on Monday, March 5, 1956, with the headline "Auto Crashes, Near Riot Give Mt. Snow Worries." The

A 1954 Vermont road map had no interstate highways. The present-day Route 100 near Mount Snow was numbered Route 8. It had gravel surface in some sections. *Author's collection.*

article reported, "Record-breaking crowds of skiers at Hogback Mountain in Marlboro and Mount Snow in West Dover, and an icy access road to Mount Snow that caused numerous accidents and a near-riot highlighted the weekend that produced some of the best skiing of the season." Reporters also blamed many drivers for having poorly treaded tires.

"The narrow access from Route 8, long a maintenance problem, was glazed by heavy traffic yesterday morning and cars were at one time backed up for over three miles from the area. Disgruntled skiers, thwarted in even reaching the area, went as far as threatening to tip over cars that were stranded across the road," the *Reformer* reported.

Mount Snow officials claimed that the funds of West Dover had run out and that the town could no longer plow and sand properly. "It has turned the blessing of snow into a liability, they claim, especially when the snow is wet and slippery," the article reported.

Days later, the *Brattleboro Reformer* said in an editorial, "With Mount Snow's attraction already demonstrated, it is about time that state authorities came to the realization that it is stupid to spend money advertising something which under current circumstances is close to unattainable. If Highway Board policy is not to spend funds on approaches to ski centers in which hundreds of thousands of dollars have been invested and whose facilities promise to contribute untold benefit to wide regions, it seems to this newspaper that it's high time that policy was changed."

The road map also provided details of Vermont's population, where farm animals living on Vermont's 19,043 farms outnumbered people. In 1954, there were 1,012,000 chickens and 489,000 cattle. The population of 377,747 humans, however, outnumbered the 332,000 turkeys in the Green Mountain State.

WALT AND THE A-BOMB

In the early 1960s, Walt Schoenknecht had another unusual idea: using an atomic bomb to create a steep vertical drop at Mount Snow. He took the proposal to the Atomic Energy Commission.

"The proposal to detonate a nuclear device on the north face of Mount Snow to develop it for skiing should not be treated entirely as a joke," noted a January 19, 1963 editorial in the *Bennington Banner*. "It was widely suspected, more than a year ago when first announced by Walt Schoenknecht, Mount Snow's president, that his idea was based more on reasons of publicity seeking than anything else."

The editorial said that a year after Schoenknecht's proposal, the AEC's Project Plowshare program was exploring peaceful uses for atomic energy. The editorial also noted a front-page *New York Times* story "accompanied by two pictures of a nuclear test blast in Nevada, which indicated, according to Dr. Edward Teller, 'father of the H-bomb,' that huge earth moving projects are feasible uses of atomic power."

The editorial continued, "Mr. Schoenknecht claims that in the Nevada test, which is said to resemble the one he proposes, 97 percent of the radioactivity was trapped. But what about that deadly three percent? How dangerous is that? What if, for instance, old Mount Pisgah is resting on the same block of granite that supports Bennington, Brattleboro, or Greenfield, Mass? Would the blast disturb buildings in those towns? Is there positive assurance that the bomb won't harm residents or homes in Dover, Wilmington, Somerset, Stratton, Searsburg, Wardsboro, and so on? The project is surely worthy of study—but plenty of it."

In the end, Walt ended up using bulldozers and some old-fashioned dynamite to cut the trails on the North Face.

WHERE THE FIRST SKIERS SPENT THE NIGHT

The lodging for Mount Snow's first skiers were village homes and farmhouses, according to the book *History of Dover*. Later, lodges were built on scenic hillsides and meadows with architectural styles ranging from Colonial to mid-Victorian to quasi–Swiss chalet.

"A radius of thirty miles has been drawn upon for lodging and food for the skiers. Devoted to the outdoors are the ski-lodge owners. Young men and women who have left professions and well-paying jobs in the cities. They have brought their families to the country to add numbers and enthusiasm to day school and Sunday school, while they themselves have added constructive participation in church and community life, as well as the inevitable problems arising at town meetings," the Dover history book noted.

Among the ski lodges in the first years of Mount Snow were Alp-Hof, the Mountaineer, Beaver Lodge, Snow and Sun, Novice Inn, Sundown Lodge, Snowflake Lodge, Snow Den, Red Cricket, Ski Haven and the Comm-on-Inn.

Prices varied depending on the style of accommodation. One of the most inexpensive ski weeks cost eighty-nine dollars per person, according to a 1974 Mount Snow ad in the *Hartford Courant*. The ski week included lift tickets, two meals daily and accommodations for five days at the "dorm-style hotel" at the Snow Barn.

Lodging at "the luxurious" Snow Lake Lodge cost more. The lodge's ski weeks had a 3:30 p.m. Sunday check-in and Friday morning check-out. A 1975 brochure listed five nights lodging, lift tickets, breakfast, "entertainment and dancing to the Paul Waldron Trio" starting at $152.75. The Snow Lake Lodge also had its famous Japanese Dream Pools, located in a tropical garden.

The Snow Lake Lodge was considered one of the more luxurious places to stay. The lodge had Japanese Dream Pools located in a tropical garden. *Author's collection.*

There were also après-learn-to-ski weeks that "packs a lot of fun into the nighttime," according to the brochure. "A welcome party, ski films, video replay of your skiing and other get-togethers." The Snow Barn no longer has overnight lodging, but it does offer live entertainment, dance parties, some food and the opportunity to meet other Mount Snow visitors.

Mount Snow's reputation as a good place to learn to ski in the 1970s also brought boxing champion Muhammad Ali to the southern Vermont resort in March 1970, according to the *Burlington Free Press*. At the time, Ali had been banned from boxing as punishment for his 1967 refusal to be inducted in the U.S. Army. He lost his heavyweight boxing title after being convicted of draft evasion.

Bob Gratton, his ski instructor at Mount Snow at that time, told the *Free Press* in a June 14, 2016 article that despite some falls and almost hitting a fence on the Mixing Bowl slope, eventually Muhammad Ali became comfortable on his skis. "On a one-on-one basis, Muhammad was a wonderful person."

BUILDING MOUNT SNOW'S LODGES, HOTEL

Walt Schoenknecht recruited another New Haven Ski Club member to design Mount Snow's lodges and test its ski lifts. His name was Everett Lord-Wood of West Hartford, Connecticut.

In World War II, Lord-Wood was a member of the U.S. Army ski troops in the Tenth Mountain Division. At the division's winter camp in Fort Hale, Colorado, he was a ski instructor for new recruits, who were taught military training in winter survival and warfare. The Tenth Mountain Division also made many contributions to skiing, including helping design and test the original snow cats to get troops and heavy equipment across mountains.

After the war, Lord-Wood became a civil engineer, designer and planner who started his own business in 1957, according to a February 26, 1967 *Hartford Courant* article. Like Schoenknecht, Lord-Wood served as president of the New Haven Ski Club.

"Schoenknecht asked his help in launching Mt. Snow," according to the *Courant* article. "Lord-Wood was receptive and designed the base lodge, Sun Lodge, Snow Lake Lodge, devised a master plan which Schoenknecht didn't follow, and supervised the testing of lifts for safety."

Lord-Wood said, "Walt designed the original lifts and patterned them after an industrial conveyor-belt system of lubricated links, very much like those used in mines" and automobile assembly plants.

Lord-Wood's design for the Sun Lodge was later used in the construction of Mohawk Mountain's base lodge in 1964. He also helped in the planning of other ski areas, including Haystack, Dorset Hollow and Bolton Valley in Vermont and Crotched Mountain in New Hampshire.

The *Courant* article with the headline "Will Skiing Jump Off the Deep End" also offered Lord-Wood's thoughts on the future of skiing and resorts. Among his predictions:

- The ski area of the future "will not be a ski area, but a 'resort community,' with the emphasis on broad appeal to the recreation market and the development of an all-season resort, all-weather facilities in an increasingly sophisticated atmosphere."
- "The new ski area will be plush compared to its predecessors. Gone will be the rope tows, the muddy parking lots, the barn-like base area. The skier of the future will be well-traveled, interested in more pleasures and comforts than a challenging run, probably accompanied by his wife and children, and

willing to pay for facilities services never thought of in the early ski areas."
- "Ski lifts will feature increased comfort through protective canopies or bubbles and greater capacity; a tremendous increase in the number of areas served by gondolas and tramways; loading and unloading will be under shelter."
- "Many facilities will be planned for non-skiers attending the area. The non-participating section of the ski-area market is of growing interest to the area manager and represents an important source of potential income."

Everett Lord-Wood lived to see most of his predictions come true. He died at age seventy-two on March 18, 1991.

WALT PROPOSES "SKI PLAZA" AT 1964–65 NEW YORK WORLD'S FAIR

After eight years of successfully operating Mount Snow, Walt Schoenknecht announced a Walt Disney–like park. A February 16, 1962 *Hartford Courant* ski column by Walt Pesko and Dot Birmingham wrote of a "New Schoenknecht Spectacular" for the 1964–65 New York World's Fair: a $3.5 million Ski Plaza:

> *The plaza would have what was billed as the world's biggest stage including a 400-foot ski slope, a 100-foot ski jump with a double chairlift and two skating rinks. The ski slope would be shaped with hand-shaped steel contours with built-in refrigeration and drainage. Snow would be chipped daily from four tons of block ice.*
>
> *Curtain for the huge stage will be a 60-foot jet spray of dancing water running the full length of a lagoon in the back of the orchestra pit. Stage effects never before attempted will be displayed. One such involves a rolling cloud effect, another a real snowstorm. A parachute ski jump will be part of a clown act.*

The plaza, the column reported, "will be slightly larger than the Yale Bowl [in New Haven, Connecticut] covered with a multi-colored aluminum roof and have seats for 5,000 spectators." Skiing would be the main feature of the ninety-minute shows, which would be staged six days a week.

"Sounds like the plaza will be the hit of the Fair and Walt is still undisputed 'King of the Hill' in ski promotion," Pesko and Donovan reported. Walt's costly Ski Plaza was never built.

Schoenknecht's success with Mount Snow preceded the development of Stratton, Killington and Sugarbush in Vermont; Waterville Valley and Loon in New Hampshire; and Hunter in New York. Many of his Mount Snow features—like wider trails, larger lodges and affordable ski weeks—would be borrowed for these other areas.

Apart from working at Mohawk and Mount Snow, Schoenknecht was also hired as a consultant to develop new ski areas in Europe and the United States. He helped develop the first ski area south of the Mason-Dixon line in Gatlinburg, Tennessee. The snowmaking system there was installed by the Larchmont Engineering Company, owned by Massachusetts brothers Phil and Joe Tropeano. The area, which opened in 1962, is now named Ober Gatlinburg. It has ten trails and a vertical drop of 850 feet.

Walt Schoenknecht was often hired as a consultant to develop new ski areas both in Europe and the United States. One was in Gatlinburg, Tennessee. *New England Ski Museum.*

In 1972, Walt Schoenknecht was asked by U.S. Senator Mike Gravel of Alaska to help develop a Mount Snow–style ski resort south of Mount McKinley (now Denali). The cost was estimated between $50 and $100 million, according to a November 13, 1972 article in the *Fairbanks Daily News-Miner*. He also proposed a never-built "Denali City" development near the mountain that would have a Teflon dome, enclosed golf courses, condos, commercial buildings and a high-speed rail line to Denali. All those plans failed to win support and action.

A more famous—and immensely successful—U.S. ski area that Walt Schoenknecht helped develop opened in 1962 in Vail, Colorado. Walt's daughter, Carol Lugar, recalled a visit there as an incredible experience. "I had gone to Vail with dad on a consulting trip when I was 12. When he and Pete Seibert [Vail's co-founder] were off creating Vail, mom and I were at the mercy of a snow cat driver who would take us to the top of something and told us to ski down and he'd be there when we got there. And then, he'd bring us back up again."

She continued, "It was a magical four or five days. It was classic Colorado; blue-sky days and powder at night. I fell in love with Vail, the area and the mountains." Lugar spent a few years working at Vail hotels, often in the evenings, so she could ski during the day.

There were other consulting trips to Europe at ski areas in Germany, Switzerland and Austria. "It was an awesome way to grow up," she said.

After working in Vail, Carol moved back east. She later worked in the Mount Snow marketing department and ended up heading it. "When things started to degrade and implode [at Mount Snow], I was more or less pushed out," she said.

In December 1968, before the first wave of Mount Snow's financial problems arrived, Walt Schoenknecht was still the king of the hill. *Brattleboro Reformer* writer John S. Hooper wrote that he "has sometimes wondered if Walt was real or simply the reincarnation of one of the ancient prophets."

Hooper wrote, "When it is said that Walt towers above the mountain it isn't because he's tall, which he is, but because what he exudes in sheer imagination is simply bigger than the mountain which wouldn't be what it is today if it were not for a dreamer who has been wired for action."

BIG PLANS UNVEILED FOR MOUNT SNOW OF THE FUTURE

On March 16, 1970, the *Bennington Banner* ran an article with the headline "Mt. Snow to Be Schoenknected into 40,000-Skiers-a-Day Vermont Fun City?"

Reporter Grady Holloway wrote a story of how Walt Schoenknecht envisioned Mount Snow twenty years into the future with a monorail, a high-rise apartment building, six cluster housing communities and "climate-controlled areas." The plan would require an additional two thousand acres for Mount Snow's development. New ski trails, chairlifts, gondolas and tramways would also be needed to accommodate an additional thirty thousand skiers.

While the Town of Dover approved $2,000 for an ecological inventory needed for planning future development, some officials questioned whether the Deerfield Valley could handle such growth.

How to pay for this future development was another big question. Schoenknecht admitted that Mount Snow "does not earn much money for the amount of money invested, but then again, 80 percent of all ski areas either break even or lose money."

The article ended, "Schoenknecht greatly relies on the hope that skiing will remain popular. In fact, he says, 'I am risking everything on it.'"

MOUNT SNOW SOLD AFTER FINANCIAL STRUGGLES

In the early 1970s, Mount Snow would see the beginning of financial struggles that would lead to new owners of the southern Vermont resort.

In January 1971, Schoenknecht sold Mount Snow to the Davos Corporation to gain more operating capital for future development. While he remained president of the ski resort, his role there steadily diminished through the 1970s. The sale was announced as a "merger" with Mount Snow becoming a wholly owned subsidiary of Davos. Among Davos's other ventures were a processor of specialty meats, seafood and prime beef, according to the *New York Times*.

On February 9, 1971, the *Brattleboro Reformer* ran a profile on Mark H. Fleischman, the thirty-one-year-old president of Davos. The headline read, "A Look at Mt. Snow's New Boss."

The Mount Snow purchase was Fleischman's second acquisition of a ski area. In 1968, Mark, his younger brother, Alan, and several New

Walt Schoenknecht was a familiar face at Mount Snow. He would be seen skiing, walking in the lodges and giving out cookies to people in lifelines. *Mohawk Mountain ski area.*

York businessmen bought the financially troubled Davos ski area in the southern Catskill Mountains for $500,000. The area was renamed Big Vanilla at Davos.

According to a 2018 article by Jeff Blumenfeld in *Skiing History*, the original Davos, named after the Swiss resort, opened in 1959. It had a 450-foot vertical drop, nineteen trails, a quad chair, a J-bar, a double chair and two T-bars. It attracted up to five thousand skiers on busy weekends. The area closed in 1991.

Mount Snow's financial problems worsened after Okuraya-Davos, Mount Snow's Japanese American parent company, filed for bankruptcy protection in the spring of 1975. The filing cited the corporation's financial plight was caused by residual debt left by the sale or liquidation of several unprofitable subsidiaries. A recession, high energy costs, a gasoline shortage in 1973 and three seasons of below-average snowfall also deepened Mount Snow's debt.

Two Mount Snow mortgages, totaling $7 million, were held by two financial trusts. Other debts were filed by unsecured creditors. Many of those creditors were owners of small businesses. First Wisconsin Mortgage Trust held the majority of the mortgages. The unsecured creditors had sought involuntary bankruptcy proceedings against Mount Snow in July but withdrew the petition three months later.

In August 1977, Preston Leete Smith, president of the Sherburne Corporation, announced the purchase of Mount Snow ski resort from the controlling owner, First Wisconsin Trust. The Sherburne Corporation also owned the Killington ski area in central Vermont. The *Rutland Herald* reported that the sale price was under $5 million. In Mohawk's early years, Smith was a ski patroller there.

Under the terms of contract, Sherburne assumed only the assets of Mount Snow, not its financial liabilities. The purchase gave Sherburne the entire Mount Snow ski resort, including two base lodges, the Snow Lake Lodge, a dormitory, the golf course, the Mount Snow airport and 1,200 acres.

"Everything Mount Snow needs, Killington's got," the *Herald* reported on August 11, 1977, "[including] the Sherburne team's management skills and Mount Snow's untapped potential for profitable growth [along] with its size and its relative proximity to the Boston and New York urban centers."

Foster Chandler, Sherburne's vice-president of marketing, said that "Mount Snow is a good ski mountain, but its facilities are not up to date as far as snow conditioning and lifts. We want to concentrate on redeveloping the skiing experience at Mount Snow by bringing the various facilities on the mountain into balance."

Under its ownership, Sherburne would remove some things that were pet projects of Schoenknecht. Gone would be the aircar from the Snow Lake Lodge, the outdoor swimming pool, the bubble gondolas, indoor skating rink and Fountain Mountain.

Carol Lugar said that when her dad lost Mount Snow, he "was pretty frustrated and my mom was pretty pissed."

In later years, Mount Snow would be owned by the American Skiing Company, Peak Resorts and, in 2019, Vail Resorts.

Decades after Walt Schoenknecht lost Mount Snow, the current owners of Mohawk Mountain (Carol Lugar and the Hedden family) still feel that he was taken advantage of in the sale of Mount Snow in 1971. "He was screwed," Lugar said. "There was an attorney and management in cahoots with Davos. The attorney was a supposed friend with my parents who was part of an organizing group selling stock."

A trail has been named after Mount Snow's founder, Walt Schoenknecht. It's located in the Sunbrook area of the southern Vermont resort. *Author's collection.*

She said in the early 1970s, "Mount Snow was in the middle of a growth spurt, and my dad was looking for money. Then the dollar fell, and it was a very rough time for anything economic."

Carol Lugar added that her mom was opposed to selling Mount Snow. "Typical of the way he was, he did it anyway. The money was the immediate solution. He was never a good businessman. He was a visionary, a dreamer, he loved the sport and did a lot to make it grow, but business savvy was not on his credentials list. And a lot of people took advantage of that."

She continued, "He wanted skiing to be the fun thing and the means to that was building [Mount Snow's] infrastructure. He wasn't the best businessman because that didn't focus on his target."

Note: If you go to Mount Snow, be sure to ski or snowboard down a blue ski trail that has a nearly eight-hundred-foot vertical drop. It offers scenic southern views and is located in the Sunbrook area of Mount Snow. Smile and stop at a sign about halfway down the trail that reads, "Thanks Walt."

DECADES BRING BOOM, BUST AND MORE SKI AREAS

In the 1960–61 season, Mohawk Mountain had its first chairlift running up the mountain. The $150,000 Boulder Bowl chair was a welcome improvement from back-aching, leg-burning rope tows that had been operating since the ski area opened in 1947.

If you wanted to ride the chairlift, a lift ticket cost $5.50; it was cheaper if you only used the rope tows. It was the first chairlift at a Connecticut ski area and had a capacity of one thousand skiers per hour.

"The new chair is not the kind originally installed at Mount Snow," the *Hartford (CT) Courant* reported on December 16, 1960. "It's an aerial cable lift made by Carlevaro and Savio of Italy. Walt Schoenknecht assured us that breakdowns would be rare and oil drippings nil."

For its fourteenth season, Mohawk also added two ponds at the top of the mountain "to feed its artificial snow apparatus which can now service a broad slope from summit to base plus a beginner slope," the *Naugatuck (CT) Daily News* reported on January 7, 1961.

Oddly, the story of Mohawk's new chairlift was picked up by the *Arizona Republic* newspaper, but it had the wrong location of the ski area. "Connecticut's East Haven ski operation on Mohawk Mountain bids strongly for a comeback in the face of stiff competition from northern New England in 1960–61 reports the New England Ski Council."

Over the next five years, Mohawk planned to add three double chairs and expand snowmaking. One of those new chairs would be the yellow-colored Mohawk double chair that premiered in 1961.

Walt and Peg's daughter, Carol Lugar, remembered the old rope tow in a July 2001 interview with the *Lakeville Journal*. "The tow ropes were powered by vehicle engines at the base stations of each tow. She recalled as a little girl helping to haul containers of gasoline that were strapped to a toboggan up the rope tows to the tow stations. This hauling had to be done frequently because the old engines were hardly fuel efficient."

The 1960–61 ski season got off to a welcome start with a December 12, 1960 blizzard that left seventeen inches of snow in Norfolk, Connecticut. Then, on January 19, 1961, a blizzard dropped nearly two feet of snow in Litchfield County. The blizzard came one day before John F. Kennedy was sworn in as the thirty-fifth president. Eight inches of snow had fallen in Washington, D.C.

That first chairlift in 1961 followed the same route as the current Boulder Summit Triple chair that ends at the top of the Timber and Wildwood trails. Between those two trails is the former path of the tandem rope tows. It's now called Chute, Mohawk's narrowest ski trail, which drops more than three hundred feet from the summit. Chute is a fun trail to ski or snowboard. Bordered by hardwood trees, it is a straight shot down the mountain. Because it's narrow, it requires short turns.

Mohawk had a Native American cartoon character (no longer used today) in its early brochures. This one, from the 1960–61 season, promoted its first chairlift and expanded snowmaking. *Mohawk Mountain ski area.*

A section of another old rope tow route is near the Indian Crossing trail at the right of the Mohawk triple chair just before it ends at the top. Up until the early 1990s, there was a small, weathered shack and remains of a rope tow wheel on the lower Pine slope.

Another relic of the ski area's early history is a small stone tower near the top of the Pinnacle trail, built nearly one hundred years ago by the Civilian Conservation Corps during the Great Depression. The tower remains in good shape.

A rope tow pulls skiers near the top of the Mohawk Mountain ski area's Pine trail in the early 1950s. *Mohawk Mountain ski area.*

Inside Mohawk's lodge, constructed in 1964, are collections of old skis, photos and large painted trail maps created by Peg Schoenknecht. Outside the main lodge, above the ticket windows, there's even a message from Mohawk's founder. It reads, "Welcome to Mohawk. Please enjoy what we have to offer. Walt Schoenknecht."

Mohawk opened about ten years before what would become an explosion in the number of skiers and, later, snowboarders.

Longtime *SKI Magazine* editor John Fry wrote in his book *The Story of Modern Skiing* that in the decades of the 1950s and 1960s, participation in

At the top of the Mohawk and Pinnacle ski trails is a small stone tower built by Civilian Conservation Corps crews in the 1930s. *Author's collection.*

Mohawk Mountain ski instructors line up in front of the main lodge in the mid-1960s. *Mohawk Mountain ski area.*

skiing grew 15 percent annually. "The engine of skiing's expansion in the 1960s was driven by demographics. The sport was inundated with young people born during the post–World War II baby boom. Here was an activity of speed and risk perfectly matched to the age of the population bubble. It also helped that society perceived skiing as a socially desirable, positive, and a healthy outdoor activity."

The rapid growth of skiing hit full throttle in the '60s. Among them was the Central Connecticut State College Ski Club in New Britain with more than one hundred members. Initially, the club's biggest problem was not having enough ski equipment. The club asked for used ski gear to repair and recondition for its members.

CONNECTICUT GETS MORE SKI AREAS

In the 1960s, Mohawk Mountain experienced increased competition from new Connecticut ski areas. All would have the snowmaking machines that Schoenknecht, the Tey engineers from Milford, Connecticut, and the Larchmont Engineering brothers pioneered to develop.

By 1964, there were 468,000 skiers in New England and 10 million across the nation waiting for the start of the ski season. "The whole picture of New England skiing has changed radically over the years. Not too long ago, skiing was the exclusive sport of pink-faced youngsters who slept in bunks and were ruggedly determined to face any discomfort for a few glorious hours of spurting down the slopes," the *Hartford Courant* reported.

The year 1964 also saw an increase in the number of chairlifts, T-bars and tows at New England ski areas. There was also an increase in the number of areas adding snowmaking and offering night skiing.

Newspapers were filled with ads intended to get people to the slopes. The Fallsview Hotel in Ellenview, New York, offered a "Swinging Singles Weekend" for young adults with cocktail parties, an indoor pool and health club and "three great bands…the le jazz hot trio." The Hayes Liner of West Hartford, Connecticut, offered charter buses to ski areas in the United States and Canada driven by "fully insured, courteous and competent drivers."

Cannon Mountain pitched its "Ambi-Ski" scene, saying that it was "uniquely equipped to delight the skier and non-skier" with "snow, trails, lifts and expert coaching from the Paul Valar Ski School for the skier…and more 'joie-de-vivre' [joy of living] for the ski-less sociable."

Otis Ridge, just over the Connecticut border in Massachusetts, offered three lifts and "a snowmaker." The ad read, "Weekdays are more fun than two barrels of monkeys."

A December 6, 1964 ski guide in the *Hartford Courant* reported, "Connecticut will be ready to offer more skiing, more conveniently, and at a more moderate cost. Skiing continues to grow at a rapid pace but nowhere faster than in Connecticut."

Unlike the earlier ski hills opened in the 1940s and '50s by ski clubs, park and rec departments or farmers, these areas were one-stop ski areas that offered trails, chairlifts, rentals, lessons and food. Many were located not far from major highways.

By the 1963–64 season, Connecticut ski areas included Mohawk, Powder Hill (now Powder Ridge Mountain Park) in Middlefield and Satan's Ridge (now Ski Sundown) in New Hartford. There was also Tapawingo in Woodbury, Mount Hope in Mansfield and the Brooklyn ski area in eastern Connecticut, all of which are now closed.

"The newest developing ski area of sizable proportions is the Mount Southington area," reported a December 6, 1964 *Hartford Courant* article. "This area promises to develop into one of the more interesting in Connecticut."

To build up excitement, a winter sport show attracted hundreds of skiers in Meriden. A fashion show of ski clothing was called "a huge success" by *Meriden (CT) Journal* ski writer Barbara Holroyd. "The Ski-Look is everywhere, as Ski Lodges become more glamourous, so do the clothes both on and off the slopes," Holroyd wrote in her December 19, 1963 ski column.

"Gay colors, stretch fabrics and the long apres-ski skirts are the real scene stealers this year. Men's parkas and pants have taken on a new look…slim stretch jackets are very popular and come in many colors. Stretch pants should be trim and if yours aren't, take them to the nearest tailor and be in style," she wrote.

Holroyd said the addition of new Connecticut ski areas offers a good variety of areas within a few miles of that "overused" easy chair. "What could be more rewarding than praise from that cute Austrian ski instructor after a successful lesson? Promise yourself this year you will get on the bandwagon and take up skiing. Your only regret will be that you didn't do it before. Where should you start? Right here in Connecticut."

TWO BROTHERS OPEN POWDER HILL IN MIDDLEFIELD

Powder Hill, now Powder Ridge Mountain Resort, opened in 1959. It was started by brothers Louis and Herman Zemel, who owned appliance stores in New Haven and Bridgeport, Connecticut. Before deciding on developing Powder Hill, Lou Zemel had proposed ski areas on West Rock in New Haven and West Peak in Meriden. Plans for those areas were rejected by local officials.

For the first three seasons at Powder Hill, there were just surface lifts. Facing competition from more Connecticut ski areas, the Zemel brothers had double chairlifts added in 1963 and 1965.

Before the 1964–65 ski season, manager Lou Zemel told the *Hartford Courant* that eighteen more chairs had been ordered to increase the lift capacity to one thousand skiers per hour. He also said that safety bars would be added, as well. "I don't agree," he told the *Courant*. "I believe chairs without bars are safer on a small hill, especially for novices. However, by popular demand, I agreed to install them."

In later years, the Zemels' ski area was the first area in New England to install a four-person chairlift. The area also experimented with unusual hours for skiing, including early bird skiing at 6:30 a.m. (with a breakfast included) and night owl skiing to 3:00 a.m. They also made their own snowmaking machines in a sub-business called Fan Jet.

Powder Ridge is also known as the site of the "Festival That Never Happened." The music festival was scheduled for July 31–August 2, 1970. Some of the performers who appeared at the Woodstock music festival a year earlier—Janis Joplin, Richie Havens and Joe Cocker—were on the Powder Ridge festival lineup.

A legal injunction filed by the Town of Middlefield blocked the festival from happening, but it didn't stop an estimated thirty thousand people showing up anyway. The only headliner performer who defied the injunction and showed up was Melanie (Safka), who scored a big hit with the song "Candles in the Rain" in April 1970.

Local bands also played at the renamed "People's Pop Festival of Powder Ridge" from makeshift stages at opposite ends of the ground, the *Hartford Courant* reported on August 3, 1970. Among the bands was Goodhill, an eight-piece group with horns and conga sections from Fairfield, Connecticut. "The band's head engineer hooked up the system to the Mister Softee [ice cream truck] generators and the sound, while not always clear, was loud enough to reach everyone on the slope."

The would-be festival also received international press coverage. An August 3, 1970 article in the *Western Daily Express* in Bristol and Avon, England, carried the headline "Drug Crisis at Pop Festival That Wasn't." The article by an unnamed "special correspondent" reported that "drug pushers reportedly have openly set up business on the roads around the grounds. Drug-taking is rife and Dr. William Abruzzi, who is in charge of cases, said the situation on the 300-acre mountain site was growing to crisis proportions."

The article reported that "among the drugs being sold openly was MDA, which acts as a love potion."

MOUNT SOUTHINGTON OPENS ON OLD DAIRY FARM

On December 12, 1964, the Mount Southington ski area opened with two T-bars and rope tows capable of carrying five thousand skiers per hour up its three trails and five slopes. The area was started by Dr. Harold Richman, Dr. Marino Grimaldi, the Palmisano family and local investors.

On December 12, 1964, the Mount Southington ski area opened with two T-bars and rope tows. The ski area was built on an old dairy farm. *New England Ski Museum.*

Richman was inspired to build a family-oriented ski area in Connecticut after a ski trip to Vermont in the early 1960s. The ski area, once a dairy farm, still uses the old barn as a cafeteria and the original farmhouse for offices and ticket sales.

Before opening in 1964, manager Walter Ayre told the *Meriden Journal* that continual skiing from the beginning of freezing temperatures until spring would be the key to the new ski area. "An elaborate snow-making system will ensure that all three trails and four slopes are available for the convenience of our skiers."

A faster and more convenient drive to Mount Southington came in the mid-1960s when Interstate 84 opened.

SATAN'S RIDGE STARTS SEASON IN NEW HARTFORD

The Satan's Ridge ski area, now Ski Sundown in New Hartford, Connecticut, started its first season on January 11, 1964, with a double chair serving its main slope with a thirty-degree angle at some points. The ski area was started by Frank Linnel, Russel Smith and Harold Law. Large bulldozers were used to clear boulders, and young boys were used to remove small stones, rocks and debris from the trails.

In July 1969, former Mohawk Mountain manager Channing Murdock and his brother, Robert, purchased the sixty-one-acre ski area and renamed it Ski Sundown. The Murdocks also owned the Butternut ski area in Great Barrington, Massachusetts.

In the 1970s, night skiing was added, more trails opened and Connecticut's first triple chairlift was installed. In 1978, Rick Carter, Sundown's general manager, purchased the area. Carter would own the area until 2002, when Robert Switzgable, a Sundown employee for nineteen years, acquired the ski area. One year later, Sundown had Connecticut's first terrain park.

In 2014, Ski Sundown opened a new double black diamond trail. Harkening back to the area's earlier name, the trail is called Satan's Stairway. The combination of Satan's Stairway and Gunbarrel gives Sundown the steepest trails in Connecticut.

SMALL TAPAWINGO SKI AREA OPENS IN WOODBURY

There was also Tapawingo, a small ski area in Woodbury founded by Kermit Adams and Thomas Brownell. It opened in the 1963–64 ski season with a rope tow and a T-bar. The name Tapawingo was derived from the Mohawk tribe's word for "Place of Joy."

Before the 1972–73 season, Rod Taylor, a former member of the U.S. Ski Team, bought the area and renamed it the Woodbury Ski and Racquet Club. Taylor later added summer attractions, including tennis courts, zip lines, a climbing wall and outdoor reggae festivals. The reggae concerts, in particular, riled neighbors in rural Woodbury.

Using money from his father's inheritance, Taylor also expanded snowmaking. For years, Taylor's small ski area was the first to open in New England. Although skiing was very limited, he took pride in beating Killington in Vermont for the first skiing of the season.

In an article I wrote about Taylor for *SKI Magazine*, he said, "Everything I've owned, I've put back. I've never ever taken a salary. To a businessperson it's a money loser." He added, "The best days are the days when you've just made snow and it's sunny. People come up to you and say the skiing is great."

Taylor died on July 5, 2014. Woodbury's last day of skiing was in March 2016. Shortly afterward, the thirty-eight-acre area was put up for sale.

MOHAWK GETS BOOST FROM *NEW YORK DAILY NEWS*

In the late 1960s and early 1970s, Mohawk started to see an uptick in New York City area skiers showing up at its slopes. A January 23, 1970 ski column in the *New York Daily News* likely helped because of its large circulation.

"In Connecticut's northwest, where the terrain begins to resemble mountains, there is a ski area that has been in existence for more than 15 years but apparently has been kept under wraps. It's Mohawk Mountain in the heart of the Mohawk State Forest, just off Route 4 in Cornwall," the article noted.

"Since its owner Walt Schoenknecht, major domo of Mt. Snow, the flourishing Vermont resort, one might expect Mohawk to be headed in the same direction. But Mohawk has built a solid reputation as a family ski area and that's the way it will stay. There are no overnight accommodations nearby and the serenity of the state forest has yet to be shattered by the beat of the new generation. Skiers who know Mohawk have wisely kept it to themselves for years and you can't blame them. It offers some fine skiing over a wide variety of trails up to a mile and a half in length, all walled off with stately pines."

MORE SLOPES OPEN IN MASSACHUSETTS

Connecticut skiers looking for longer trails and a steeper vertical drop would drive a little longer into Massachusetts to some of the following sites.

BUTTERNUT BASIN. In 1963, former Mohawk Mountain manager Channing Murdock and his wife, Jane, opened Butternut Basin at the site of the former G-Bar-S ranch site in Great Barrington. It offered a 4,100-foot chairlift and added trails, rope tows, snowmaking and a modern ski lodge designed by Hartford Ski Club member Rene Burdet of Granby. In August 1962, the Murdocks purchased the old ranch that first offered skiing and two rope tows in the 1939–40 season. Additional rope tows were added for the 1941–42 season.

Butternut opened on December 24, 1963, two days and a month after the assassination of President John F. Kennedy in Dallas, Texas.

Murdock spent two seasons at Mohawk Mountain learning the ins and outs of running a ski area from Walt Schoenknecht. Like Schoenknecht did with Connecticut officials, Channing Murdock secured an agreement with Massachusetts to lease state forestland for his ski area.

In 1989, Murdock returned to Mohawk Mountain to help the ski area recover from a July 10 tornado that caused $2.5 million in damage to lifts, buildings and infrastructure. On May 29, 1995, Murdock would face the same fate as Mohawk when a tornado knocked down trees, damaged five lifts and caused more than $2 million in damage. Three people were killed when the automobile they were in was lifted several hundred feet in the air and then dropped in a wooded hillside, according to the National Weather Service's storm event database. Debris from the tornado was found forty-five miles away in Belchertown, Massachusetts, where a racing ticket from the Great Barrington Fairgrounds was found.

BRODIE MOUNTAIN. A new ski area located near Walt and Peg Schoenknecht's first rope tow area in New Ashford, Massachusetts opened in the 1964–65 season. A four-thousand-foot chairlift gave skiers access to some of the steepest and longest trails in the Berkshires.

MOUNT TOM. The Holyoke, Massachusetts ski area added something different for the 1964–65 season: night skiing "with the most up-to-date lighting systems in the country," reported the *Morning Record* of Meriden. "The system is the brightest that is possible to install for outdoor use and gives even distribution on an entire slope area."

WALT SCHOENKNECHT:
MOHAWK "A SPECIAL PET" FOR ME

In the mid-1970s, after nearly two decades of success, Mohawk founder Walt Schoenknecht's dream ski resort—Mount Snow in Vermont—would start to melt away with increasing financial problems. It would begin in 1971 when Davos assumed day-to-day operations and financial oversight of the resort.

Walt Schoenknecht remained the de facto face of Mount Snow for a few years, until the Sherburne Corporation acquired Mount Snow on August 8 1977. Sherburne, headed by Killington founder Preston Smith, paid $4.5 million for the resort, according to I. William Berry's *Great North American Ski Book*. Smith and Killington co-founder Joseph Sargeant had skied at Mohawk Mountain in its early years.

Twenty years after Mohawk installed a snowmaking system and seven years before Mount Snow's sale, Walt Schoenknecht reflected on the Connecticut ski area's development. "I want our skiers to know that it [Mohawk] is still very much a special pet of mine," he told *Bridgeport Post* ski editor Ken Maloney.

> *We are trying for facilities that will be second only to Mount Snow.*
>
> *I tried to create a model for a middle-sized resort with our base lodge and had lots of fun designing it. We like to think that it is different with its tremendous sun decks built out over and between three small ponds and brooks, with the arched bridge leading through the pines to the lifts.*
>
> *We tried to keep Mohawk a friendly place. I am not here as much as I would like, but I hope skiers will say hello to my wife Peg, or Steve Hedden, our manager, or his mother, Edna, who manages the lodge. The Heddens have been with us since the beginning, as have our shop and ticket people.*

Like Mount Snow, Mohawk Mountain also had a frozen geyser near its base lodge. *Author's collection.*

Maloney's interview with Schoenknecht was in January 1970. Mohawk had just finished installing its third double chairlift and replaced the upper rope tow with a Poma lift. "This now gives us a wide range of lifts with something for all skiers. One double chairlift is for novices, the Poma lift that goes three-quarters of the way up the mountain for intermediates, and we still have seven rope tows so that waiting, even on the weekends, is held down."

He continued, "We have tried to keep our prices as low as we can, especially in these days of high expense. Any weekday has a much lower priced ticket and the special ladies' day ticket on Wednesday at one half-price is really popular. We like youth and have worked with a number of youth groups and schools on a special basis."

How much were lift tickets in 1970? On weekends, for all lifts, $6.50; a weekday ticket was $5; and the ladies' day ticket was $2.50.

Decades before the concern of global warming, ski area operators were fighting to stay in business despite the weather. The year 1973 was not a good snow year. Mohawk manager Steve Hedden said at the time that "it was probably the worst winter in a long, long time," according to a United Press International article. He said that Mohawk closed two weeks earlier than normal. "The thing is, you learn to take the good with the bad," Hedden said, recalling 1970 as "a very good snow year."

The Mohawk double chairlift debuted in the 1960–61 ski season. The chair runs alongside the Mohawk ski trail, carved in 1939. *Author's collection.*

In 1978, Mohawk celebrated its thirtieth anniversary. Walt Schoenknecht said in a February 2 article in the *Lakeview Journal*, "Mohawk has found a new future. From what I see now, the economic situation along with inflation is such that people will have to curtail their weekend trips to Vermont or north to ski resorts. What we hope to do is fill the gap and make Mohawk a weekend ski retreat."

Schoenknecht said he hoped to see "Mohawk developed into a model resort and above all, to keep it a friendly family place." He added, "We are pleased and proud to have many of the original employees still with us." Edna Hedden, the lodge manager since the area opened in the first season, was honored with flowers and a pewter plate from the Mohawk staff and ski patrol.

Edna Hedden also served as spokesperson for Mohawk. In January 1981, she was happy that Mohawk was getting some natural snow. "Last year the whole season was lousy," she said. "Seeing snow in the backyard brings people to the slopes. The average person doesn't know machines."

Many longtime Mohawk skiers likely talked to Edna. For many years, she was the woman who sold lift tickets in the main lodge.

In February 1997, *Hartford Courant* columnist Owen Canfield interviewed Edna when she was eighty-one. She told him that she was "forever

Cornwall….I live in the most beautiful part of Cornwall and on the most beautiful street, Cherry Street. I hear the claim that Norfolk is Connecticut's icebox. I smile. It's always colder here."

In 1997, ski areas were again struggling with a mild winter. "That's the way winters are," she said. "I remember one winter in the Forties I think, early Fifties, in which we were only open one-half day the whole winter. When you have a business that depends on the weather, well that's how it is, especially in New England."

She continued, "Last year, we had a great winter for skiing, yet we had six and a half inches of rain in January. You wouldn't realize that because of all the snow. Did you know—I bet you didn't—that snowmaking was born right here at Mohawk? It's true. We still make and groom the best snow. And by the way, this is the oldest, biggest ski area in the state. And, as I said, the coldest."

SCHOENKNECHT INDUCTED IN SKI HALL OF FAME

In 1979, Walt Schoenknecht was inducted into the U.S. Ski and Snowboard Hall of Fame. In Walt's induction letter by ski writer I. William Berry, there was no mention of Schoenknecht's role in the development of a snowmaking machine or the creation of Mohawk Mountain.

"Does Walter Schoenknecht need an introduction?" Berry wrote. "Does Mount Snow need a description? They shouldn't. If there is any man and any mountain to which a generation of intermediate skiers owe a massive debt of thanks, it's these two."

He continued, "Some years ago, the idea of a 'great ski mountain' was a maze of tight, steep, twisty trails facing north—a complex to chill even the experts and to petrify the intermediates. Before Walter, skiing was hardship and survival: Mansfield, Cannon, Mad River Glen and rough-hewn base lodges heated by pot-belly stoves. A great wave of nostalgia sweeps over us as we think of those days—but for too many, it's too much. Then Walter drifted in West Dover, Vermont and saw Reuben Snow's farm and the big rolling lump that towered above it. That day, a new era was formed. All Walter did, when you come down to it, was to make skiing fun for all levels of skiers."

Schoenknecht's induction in the Hall of Fame came a few years after he lost Mount Snow. Berry mentioned Mount Snow's wide trails, open slopes,

In 1979, Walt Schoenknecht, *left*, was inducted into the U.S. Ski and Snowboard Hall of Fame. *U.S. Ski and Snowboard Hall of Fame.*

two-person gondolas, Oriental pools and clock tower terminals. "And it was all Walter's…it was all Walter."

At the end of the induction letter, Berry wrote, "Greatness? He owned no gold medals, but he owned a record anyone would love to have. Fighting serious physical illness and corporate fiscal woes and suspecting he had little chance to regain control of his mountain, he never looked back, as many might have, to those 'good old days.' Knowing that Sherburne's takeover was imminent (although never letting on), that his four-million-dollar fortune had vanished, his only thoughts were for the future of the mountain. Perhaps his vision, as always, would turn an environmentalist pale, but would make a skier sing."

DEATH OF A SKI PIONEER AND TRAILBLAZER

In the early 1980s, Carol Lugar became a full-time vice-president of Mohawk Mountain Ski Area Inc. She earlier worked in Vail, Colorado, and at Mount Snow in Vermont.

She became president of Mohawk Mountain when her father announced his retirement weeks before his death from prostate cancer on October 30, 1987. Steve Hedden, Edna's son, became vice-president when Lugar left the position.

Peg Schoenknecht would remain as a director of Mohawk Mountain until her death on July 29, 2008, at age ninety.

Walter Robert Schoenknecht died on October 30, 1987, at age sixty-eight. *Mohawk Mountain ski area.*

In a November 25, 1987 article in the *Lakeville Journal,* Lugar said that she was comfortable in her increased responsibilities. "I've been acting in this capacity on a full-time basis for a number of years and I've got Steve to help me."

She said that after her dad's death, skiers "won't see a great deal of changes this season." The renovation of snowmaking lines, the base lodge and fuel storage tanks were among the few modifications. "Mohawk, the nation's pioneering snowmaking mountain, is making snow and the (outside ice) fountain is growing," Lugar said.

TORNADOS RAVAGE MOHAWK MOUNTAIN

Monday, July 10, 1989, was the Mohawk Mountain ski area's "Day of Infamy." Just before 4:30 p.m., a series of destructive tornados tore through a portion of the ski lodge, destroyed a maintenance building, twisted chairlifts, damaged equipment and toppled towering pine trees. The damage, estimated at more than $2.5 million, was so severe many doubted the ski area would be open for the 1989–90 ski season.

The day after Thanksgiving, Mohawk did open that season, but getting back on a solid financial footing would take more than a decade. It also took a four-year court battle to get Mohawk's insurance company to pay up.

Carol Lugar, Mohawk's co-owner and president, remembers the day well. "I had driven my daughter down to friends in Kent. I was driving back up along the Housatonic River and remember looking to the west and thinking that it's a weird looking sky, starting to turn green, like a nasty thunderstorm."

Once safely inside her house, she looked outside and saw the sky getting darker. "The thing I remember most, I had a row of big oak trees in front of the house. I remember looking at them through the window and they were swaying in the wind and remember thinking I didn't know a tree that big could bend without breaking. And literally, in the blink of an eye, they were all shattered. Then, there was a lull and then another significant pass of a strong storm."

Once the storm passed, Lugar went outside and scrambled down a bank to check on a neighbor, who was unharmed.

On July 10, 1989, tornados destroyed a maintenance building, twisted chairlifts, damaged equipment and toppled towering pine trees. *Mohawk Mountain ski area.*

"I looked down the road and it was just trees across everywhere and I knew that I couldn't do much. I couldn't see the maintenance building [at the ski area]."

Before the tornado struck, brothers Don and Brad Hedden were at Mohawk working on a lift, preparing to change a bearing. They are sons of then Mohawk general manager Steve Hedden.

"The guys remarked about the darkening sky and the impending storm, and Don said he was going down to the store to get a pack of cigarettes before the storm hit. He had recently taken up smoking—maybe a pack a month," said his father, to keep the bugs away," according to a September 1989 article in *Ski Area Management*. "Brad told him to go ahead, that he would keep working and get everything ready to go first thing in the morning."

"No, c'mon with me," Don said. "We'll talk to the guys at the gas station for a few minutes. Then we'll come back." That decision to go to the store together likely saved the Hedden brothers' lives. The building they were in before leaving was destroyed.

Lugar, who walked to the store about a mile from her house, was relieved to see the Heddens. She was told that the ski area was "Gone, gone, gone," she recalled. "There were at least two [tornados], possibly as many as five in the valley and that was from the National Weather Service," she said.

Ben Waller, who lives about two miles from the ski area, said he was returning from Maine when he saw the tornado damage. Because of many downed trees, he was forced to walk to his house from the four-corner intersection of Route 4 and 43. "I started walking to my house and everything was fine until I got to the driveway of Mohawk. I looked over and

This aerial photo shows the extensive damage caused by a series of tornados. It caused $2.5 million in damage. *Mohawk Mountain ski area.*

the entire ski area was mangled. All the trees were laid down in one direction going sideways. The pile of trees was about six or seven feet tall; it was like a logging truck dumped the trees."

Waller said he saw ski lift chairs strewn around the towers. "The chairlifts were wrapped around them all tied in knots. The tornado destroyed the lower half of the mountain from the Nutmeg slope to all the way half up the Arrowhead trail."

According to the *Lakeview Journal,* "One of the 21-ton counterweights which makes the ski lift line taut was pulled all the way up its tower, threatening to let go of the entire haul rope that holds the chairs [about one hundred chairs per lift]."

After the tornados, many did not expect the ski area to open for the 1989–90 season. Volunteers helped Mohawk open the day after Thanksgiving. *Mohawk Mountain ski area.*

Days after the tornado, ski area operators from New England and New York were among the many volunteers who went to Mohawk Mountain to help. "We had such tremendous support, particularly from the ski industry and customers," said Lugar. "Our ski patrol was out here cleaning up debris, people who had skied here for years came out and helped. It was all pretty much volunteers, people who had some history with us." Ski areas also pitched in to help by repairing damaged machinery and sending badly needed parts.

A decision by one of the world's most famous rock bands kept them out of the path of the tornado. Weeks before the tornados struck, Lugar said, the Rolling Stones expressed interest in using the Mohawk Mountain ski lodge for rehearsals for their upcoming Steel Wheels tour in the United States. "They liked the acoustics" of the lodge, she said.

Lugar said Mohawk was one of three venues the band considered in northwest Connecticut. The band later selected the former Wykeham Rise Girls' School, giving them shelter in Washington, Connecticut, about a dozen miles south of Mohawk.

With winds ranging between 100 to 175 miles per hour, the tornados also destroyed 70 percent of Cathedral Pines, Connecticut's oldest-growth forest and longtime tourist attraction. Some of the two-hundred-year-old white pines stood 150 feet tall, creating a dark canopy. The effects of the tornado at Cathedral Pines can still be seen today off Essex Hill Road; a trail traverses the last remaining intact part of the stand, according to the Nature Conservancy.

Cathedral Pines is just over the western ridge from the ski area. According to a July 23, 1989 article in the *Record-Journal* of Meriden, Connecticut, dairy farmer Frank Calhoun donated the forty-two acres of the Cathedral Pines to the Nature Conservancy.

"My sister and I were getting older, and we wanted to make sure the trees were preserved," Calhoun told the *Record-Journal*. He said his father purchased the land in 1883 to protect the pines from lumber companies. "It's hard to believe that what nature took hundreds of years to build, it can also destroy in just one evening," Calhoun said.

PATH OF THE TORNADOS

In 1989, the National Weather Service rated a tornado's wind speed and damage on the Fujita Scale, or F-Scale: F-0 (under 73 mph winds, with light damage), F-1 (73–112 mph winds, with moderate damage), F-2 (113–157 mph winds, with considerable damage), F-3 (158–206 mph winds, with severe damage), F-4 (207–260 mph winds, with devastating damage) and F-5 (261–318 mph winds, with incredible damage). The Fujita Scale was replaced on February 1, 2007, with the more accurate Enhanced Fujita Scale, or EF Scale.

According to the National Oceanic and Atmospheric Administration, the July 10, 1989 tornado caused damage in three separate segments between one and one and a half miles each along a ten-mile-long path. The F2 tornado began in the Salisbury, Connecticut area and had a width of seventy-three yards, according to NOAA's Storms Events Database.

"In the Cornwall area, along the first 1.5-mile segment, the tornado caused severe damage to the Mohawk Mountain Ski Lodge and caused over 2 million dollars' worth of damage in the sparsely populated vicinity. Also destroyed was 'Cathedral Pines,' a historically significant forest which was a National Landmark."

Downed trees closed Route 4 between Route 128 and Route 125 in Cornwall. While no serious injuries were reported in Cornwall Village, several people were cut by flying glass. Strong winds knocked down the top of the steeple of Cornwall's United Church of Christ on Bolton Hill Road. In nearby Goshen, two cows and a bull were crushed when a barn collapsed. Trees were stripped of bark and leaves.

"The tornado moved in a south-southeast direction and caused significant tree damage along its second segment of the damage path, about one mile long, in Milton. Hundreds of felled trees blocked most roads in Milton. In its third and final damage path section, the tornado caused major destruction along a 1.5-mile path through the town of Bantam. The only building left entirely intact in the small town was the fire station."

The NOAA database also lists another F2 tornado that traveled five miles from Litchfield to New Haven Counties. The width of the tornado was one hundred yards. "The tornado touched down in Watertown (at 3:17 p.m.) and moved into Oakville. Fifty homes received heavy damage and hundreds more sustained less serious damage. Hundreds of trees were knocked down, blocked roads and felled utility wires."

Jennifer Bike, twelve, of Stratford, Connecticut, was killed on a church camping trip at Black Rock State Park when a tree fell on her tent. Also injured was her sixteen-year-old sister, Melanie, and two other campers. Melanie Bike was paralyzed from her injuries, a broken neck and damaged spinal cord. The Bike family later sued the State of Connecticut, claiming it was negligent because park workers were not adequately trained to spot dangerous weather and warn campers of possible danger.

As the tornado continued into Waterbury, a church steeple was knocked down, several buildings had their roofs ripped off and several warehouses were leveled. At least fifty people received mainly minor injuries. The tornado dissipated within the city of Waterbury.

NOAA said that the thunderstorm complex responsible for the tornados continued to move south-southeast and produced another tornado. The tornado traveled 4.6 miles from Hamden to just north of New Haven.

"This major tornado, an F4, which is rare for New England, touched down in Hamden. It devastated a portion of the community, especially a section known as Highwood. As many as 350 homes and over 40 businesses were destroyed, resulting in many hundreds of people being displaced. The more significant tornado damage was along about a 0.5-mile path, but tree damage extended much farther. Damage estimates in Hamden alone exceeded 100 million dollars. Miraculously, no deaths occurred, and injuries were rather minor," according to NOAA.

The tornado continued along an intermittent path toward the south-southeast to North Haven and ended north of New Haven. An estimated

$20 million was caused by falling trees that blocked more than thirty streets and caused major power outages, some for nearly a week.

Six weeks after the tornados, Lugar told the *Hartford Courant* damage to the ski area was an overwhelming sight, "with lots of people second-guessing us" on when Mohawk would reopen. "I think we're at the point now where we're seeing a lot of physical changes here that indicate a lot of progress. And while it's still a little dismaying-looking, there's still no doubt in our minds it [the ski area] will open on time. It's going to look different. It's not going to be as pretty. Virtually every tree in that area is either down or severely damaged."

Clearing the downed trees accelerated after the state awarded a contract to Trowbridge Land Clearing of Hampton. There was some delay in clearing the downed trees on Mohawk Mountain.

State Senator M. Adela Edds of Kent said at the time the contract was delayed because the state needed to get competitive bids for the land clearing. "Because of all the red tape Mohawk Mountain ski area has had to suffer setbacks within a month's time. Once because of Mother Nature and once because of big brother bureaucracy."

The loss of thousands of trees made Mohawk look like a barren place in the winter of 1989–90. *Mohawk Mountain ski area.*

Snowmaking turned the bare slopes of Mohawk Mountain white in December 1989. This is the area where towering pine trees once stood. *Mohawk Mountain ski area.*

After Edds visited Mohawk days after the tornado, she said, "It was horrendous; the trees were all down and the [chairlifts] were all sort of twisted around. It was just a disastrous thing."

In late November 1989, Mohawk's ski lifts passed mandatory state safety inspections and even more stringent inspections by the ski area's insurance company.

With the approaching winter season, ski shops advertised the latest ski equipment and clothing. The Ski Haus in Middletown was selling Raichle and Alpina ski boots ranging from $89 to $249. A Head ski package with skis and bindings using "Radical Air Core technology" sold for $149. Tyrolia was introducing "the world's first integrated ski and binding designed to work together to maximize flex."

The highest-priced item in the Ski Haus ad was a one-piece Skiing Finesse woman's ski suit for $365.65, discounted from $487.50.

On November 24, 1989—the day after Thanksgiving—Mohawk opened for its forty-third season. The price of an all-day lift ticket was twenty-eight dollars. "We are ready to go," Lugar said. "We're like ducks—serene on the surface but pedaling like crazy underneath."

TORNADO AFTERMATH:
MANY YEARS OF FINANCIAL STRUGGLES

Below that serene surface was a lawsuit Mohawk filed against its insurance company that would take nearly four years to settle.

In July 1991, Mohawk filed a lawsuit against the American Home Insurance Company in Litchfield Superior Court. The dispute was whether the ski area should get insurance money for the damage from the tornados.

Mohawk had purchased the weather-related policy from a New Hampshire agent for the American Home Insurance Company of New York. The policy stated the ski area was covered $650,000 "per loss." The lawsuit said that two distinct tornados hit the area, one causing $704,650 and the other causing damages totaling $935,917. The insurance company only paid $650,000 for one tornado.

"In our view it was one storm," Joseph Skelly, a lawyer affiliated with the insurance company, told the *Hartford Courant*. "I'm sure there's scientific evidence that supports the American Home position."

David Foose from the National Weather Service in Bridgeport, Connecticut, saw the damage at Mohawk in the storm's aftermath. He told the *Courant* that as many as three tornados might have struck Mohawk. But he said that identifying tornados sometimes is difficult. "It's a very inexact thing," he told the *Courant* in 1991.

Foose said to determine where a tornado hits, investigators examine the pattern of fallen trees, damage to structures, radar, aerial photos and pictures taken on the ground. Strong winds from storms can cause damage that is hard to distinguish from tornados.

The NWS investigation process had changed since 1989. NWS survey teams are now equipped with a variety of technology devices, including a GPS unit, laptops, cellphones, survey software, digital cameras, aerial surveys and satellite images.

On its side, Mohawk offered evidence and testimony that the July 10, 1989 storm damage came from two tornados less than an hour apart, each striking separate areas of the ski area. The insurance company argued that the damage incurred was the result of one storm and, thus, one occurrence.

On December 15, 1994, a jury ruled in favor of Mohawk, with a verdict of an additional $650,000 together with 10 percent interest from October 3, 1989. The insurance company's lawyers asked the court to set aside the verdict. The court later upheld the verdict ruling, stating that the insurance had a $650,000-per-occurrence policy. The ruling said, "The

Left: Peg Schoenknecht and her daughter, Carol Lugar, skiing in the early 1990s. After the 1989 tornados, Peg wanted Carol to take over the ski area. Peg continued to ski until she was eighty-one. *Mohawk Mountain ski area.*

Below: The winter after the tornados, Mohawk saw more snowboarders on its trails. In 1991, Mohawk added night skiing to help it recover financially. *Mohawk Mountain ski area.*

policy contained no generic definition of occurrence, nor did it specify what events constituted an occurrence except with respect to the perils of earthquake and flood."

Lugar said that the tornados represented "a tremendous, tremendous amount of work and a huge struggle for us. The insurance company gave us a lot of trouble; it took us four years to get through the insurance mess. It was probably a 15 to 18-year struggle for us to completely come out from under the tornado damage."

Before and after the insurance policy lawsuit, Mohawk was working to improve its finances. After the tornado, Peg wanted her daughter, Carol, to take over the ski area. There would be much work to be done to recover from the damage and fight the insurance company in court. Peg would live another nineteen years after the tornados. And she would still be skiing at eighty-one.

For the 1991–92 ski season, Mohawk offered night skiing on many of its trails. Until then, it was the only one of five Connecticut areas that didn't have skiing under the lights,

For years, Lugar said that Mohawk chose not to offer night skiing and snowboarding. "We always thought there was a connection with alcohol and night skiing. It was one of the things that held us back," she said in a December 8, 1991 *Bridgeport Post* interview. "It seemed like night skiing was more like a party kind of scene."

But she said that time—and economic conditions—changed in 1991. "In the last five years, people have become more serious; they are more concerned about exercise and their bodies." This, she believed, changed the atmosphere of night skiing. "The other reason was financial. The tornados that heavily damaged the area left us with a horrendous amount of debt."

Adding night skiing allowed Mohawk to increase its revenue by 25 to 30 percent. She said that after studying the area's demographics and talking to Mohawk's guests, she believed it was the right move at the right time. "Many of our skiers also come from two-income families and it seems the only time they have together is when it's dark. We need to be here for them."

At a meeting in September 1991 with Mohawk owners and the state Department of Environmental Protection, some of the one hundred Cornwall residents who attended raised concerns over night skiing: increased commercialization of the town, increased traffic, bright lights and noise. But DEP officials told the residents that the ski area is on leased state land and is exempt from town zoning regulations.

In May 1995, Mohawk came up with another way to raise cash: a $1,750 "Gold Pass" for unlimited skiing for ten years.

"As anyone familiar with Mohawk Mountain knows, the 1989 tornados were devastating to the facilities, the scenery and to the area's finances," the ski area's owners announced in a press release. "A dedicated crew and Mother Nature are taking care of the first two problems but recovering from the financial rebuilding costs has been a struggle. We are able to pay loans and operating expenses as we always have, but we consistently find ourselves without funds for capital improvement projects that are part of our long-term goals. The sole purpose of the Gold Pass revenues is to provide financing for those changes."

More than three decades after the tornados, tree damage can still be seen, especially in the western section of the ski area, alongside the Deer Run trail and on the ridge facing Mohawk Mountain.

HOW THE MOHAWK SKI AREA SURVIVES

What's the biggest concern the operators of the Mohawk Mountain ski area face every season? The answer is easy because it's something they've been dealing with since the area opened on December 26, 1947. It's warmer, rainy winters, less natural snow and rising temperatures.

More than seven decades since founder Walt Schoenknecht tried to battle snow-stingy winters with tons of shaved ice, and later a snowmaking machine, Mohawk's current owners are working with new technology that could give the area an edge.

Its TechnoAlpin snow machines that automatically start when temperatures, humidity and other atmospheric factors are right. Five TechnoAlpin and two SMI snow fans were added during the 2023–24 season.

From the earliest snowmaking system in 1950, today's snowmaking fans are smarter, more energy efficient and able to blow more snow and cover the most terrain. They also don't require people to flip the switch when the atmospheric sweet spot of snowmaking is reached.

"We are moving more and more to automation," Mohawk president Carol Lugar said. "We came across a couple of guns and the salesmen thought we should try them. We like them and we really liked the automation because there's really not a lot of snowmakers out there because it's a pretty grueling job. The automated machines capitalized on the current ambient weather and if they sense the weather is sufficient they come on. It's a pretty cool system."

Mohawk Mountain is Connecticut's oldest and largest ski area. At 650 feet, it has the largest vertical drop in the state. *Author's collection.*

She also said the younger Steve Hedden has taken it upon himself to retrofit some of the older snowmaking equipment with kits to automate them. Mohawk has about one hundred snowmaking guns.

Mohawk is hoping to build a significant system of automated snowmaking machines over a period of time. "We have without a doubt the most talented and dedicated group of snowmakers and groomers anywhere. So, I think it's a question of having the talent and the perseverance to make this happen. These guys work incredibly hard, work very long hours and are very dedicated in what they do."

To improve conditions on the mountain, Mohawk also added a German-made PistenBully 600 grooming machine during the 2023–24 season.

Lugar also said that Mohawk is very conscious of water management. "The nice thing about snow is we're only using it and it goes back into the watershed."

Mohawk's president added that the changing weather may ultimately make the area adapt to other sports. "We just don't know, it's an evolution and that's the way we look at it. It's not happening tomorrow, but it may change. We don't know. Mother Nature still has something to say about this of whether the moons will realign or maybe even another ice age. It's a one day at a time thing."

NON-SKIING ACTIVITIES

Unlike other ski areas, Mohawk does not offer many activities and events in the three other seasons. Mohawk rents building space for people or groups for such events as weddings, showers, corporate activities or meetings. Venues include the main lodge, the Pine Lodge and the Perch. The area has also hosted mountain bike camps and the Ironhike Endurance Challenge.

In the 1980s, Mohawk also held outdoor music concerts. On October 9, 1983, James Taylor sang at a day-long environmental festival celebrating the Housatonic River. He sang songs including "Old Man River" and "Fire and Rain," He said during the concert, "We have an administration in Washington that turns its back on all environmental issues. If we become conscious, if we become careful, we'll know in 50 years if we can live here or not."

Lugar said, "We have some new staff with different talents and there are certainly things we can do more of…it's a question of balancing the care that's required for the mountain and its parts. It's a high, high maintenance business. The biggest staff here in the summer months is maintenance. The lift maintenance alone is staggeringly time consuming. It's a summerlong grind to get it all done. We're also constantly replacing pipes, cables and wires. It's a huge undertaking, and no one ever sees the time and the cost and the effort that goes into making it run as smoothly as it does in the winter."

Mohawk's lease with the state was spotlighted during a January 2024 visit by Governor Ned Lamont and other officials. They announced the creation of the Office of Outdoor Industry and Experiences. The idea is to have

Connecticut governor Ned Lamont gets help with his boots before skiing at Mohawk Mountain. *Ken Dixon*, CT Insider, *January 12, 2024.*

the state partner with businesses and groups to provide more recreational options and services in state parks. Among the possible uses are equipment rentals and entering into long-term lease agreements.

The ski area was a good choice for the announcement because Mohawk has had a state lease for land since 1947. Initially, the lease was for 100 acres. The current thirty-year lease, approved in April 2017, is for 235 acres.

According to the state Department of Energy and Environmental Protection, "The fee schedule will be reviewed and amended at least every five years to reflect current fair market value. It is mutually agreed by both parties that, in view of the public benefit in maintaining a recreational facility at Mohawk Mountain, the fee schedule is subject to upward and/or downward revision annually upon determination of the state after consideration of economic conditions and competitive indicators with the approval of the lease."

The lease "requires annual payments to be substantiated by books, records, income tax returns prepared and certified by an independent CPA and delivered to the state by April 1."

During her visit to Mohawk with Lamont, DEEP commissioner Katie Dykes said that Mohawk paid the state about $80,000 to lease the land the previous season. Before heading for the slopes, Lamont acknowledged Mohawk's contribution to skiing, saying, "Snowmaking was made right here."

WHO OWNS MOHAWK MOUNTAIN?

Mohawk Mountain Ski Area Inc. was formed on December 15, 1964, according to the records of the Office of the Connecticut Secretary of State.

The ski area is co-owned by Carol Lugar, daughter of founders Walt and Peg Schoenknecht, and members of the Hedden family. Shares of Mohawk's ownership stocks are divided equally between the Lugar and Hedden families.

Edna Hedden was the first family member to work at Mohawk Mountain when it first opened. Her husband, Donald S. Hedden, was a self-employed dairy farmer at Cornwall's Maple Hill Farm and World War I veteran who died at age eighty-three in June 1979. Since its opening in 1947, Edna worked as a manager in the main Mohawk lodge, selling lift tickets before her death in 2007 at age ninety-one. Her son, Donald Stevenson Hedden, has been associated with Mohawk Mountain since he was three years old.

Steve Hedden, former Mohawk vice-president, and Carol Lugar on the deck of the main lodge in April 2024. *Author's collection.*

Today, there are about a dozen Hedden family members who work in year-round and seasonal positions. In the winter, Mohawk employs about four hundred people in seasonal positions.

Principals in Mohawk Mountain Ski Area Inc. include Lugar as president/treasurer, Donald Stevenson Hedden as secretary, Donald Hedden III as vice-president and Kara E. Lugar (Carol's daughter) as director.

WHAT WOULD WALT SAY TODAY?

In an interview, Lugar was asked what her father would think about Mohawk today. She said, "He'd be pleased, especially with the science and the improvements. He wouldn't be pleased by the cost; he would hate that and he would worry about the people who couldn't afford it."

Months before his death, Walt Schoenknecht wrote a letter to local ski writers. He wrote about the high costs of insurance, electric bills that were up to $80,000 a month, expensive diesel compressors and the $5 million spent in the last decade on new lifts and more snowmaking. "All of this started because snowmaking was born here at Mohawk in 1949. If our skiers realize the problems, they may realize why higher ticket costs are coming in," Schoenknecht wrote. He ended the letter by writing, "We're going to make snow here come hell or high water."

And seventy-five years after the first snowmaking machine, Mohawk is still making snow.

In this winter 2024 photo, Mohawk's snowmaking runs at full blast, covering nearly 100 percent of its terrain. *Mohawk Mountain ski area.*

TIMELINE OF MOHAWK MOUNTAIN SKI AREA AND SNOWMAKING

AUGUST 5, 1917

Margaret "Peg" Moss born in Karuizawa, Japan, daughter of American engineer Robert Faulkner Moss and Sybil Howard Moss.

MAY 2, 1919

Walter Robert Schoenknecht born in New Haven, Connecticut, the first son of German immigrants Henry and Meta Schoenknecht, owners of a fifteen-acre vegetable and tree nursery in East Haven, Connecticut.

JULY 19, 1921

State Park and Forest Commission takes possession of 867 acres on Mohawk Mountain. The land is a gift from Alain and Margaret "May" White. Beginning in 1908, the Whites bought and preserved 9,000 acres as a memorial to their parents. In total, the White Memorial Foundation contributes more than 2,900 acres to the Mohawk Mountain state park and forest.

OCTOBER 29, 1929

Start of the Great Depression in the United States after 16 million stocks are quickly sold by panicked investors who lost faith in the American economy.

MARCH 1933

Newly elected president Franklin D. Roosevelt calls Congress in an emergency session to pass the Emergency Conservation Act, creating the Civilian Conservation Corps. The CCC puts millions of unemployed young men to work. Environmental and conservation work includes planting millions of trees, building roads, constructing lodges and forest fire protection.

JUNE 23, 1933

CCC opens Camp Toumey at Mohawk Mountain.

1936–37

CCC crews turn forest roads into two ski trails in Mohawk Mountain State Forest.

1939

Under the direction of the Connecticut Winter Sports Association and State Forest Department, the first downhill ski trail is cut on Mohawk Mountain. The trail—named Mohawk—is Mohawk's oldest downhill ski trail.

1940

Walt Schoenknecht works at Chance Voight aircraft plant in Stratford, Connecticut. Factory builds thousands of F4U Corsair planes for combat in the Pacific. Also working at the plant are aviation engineers Wayne Pierce, Art Hunt and Dave Richey. Along with Schoenknecht, they would later test the first snowmaking machine for a ski area.

JANUARY 6, 1941

Quinnipiac Club, now called the New Haven Ski Club, is formed. Organized by Kriste Hille at the request of Schoenknecht and Marjorie Zang, who works at the YMCA. Shortly afterward, Walt meets Peg Moss, his future wife, at a club event.

JULY 26, 1941

CCC's Camp Toumey in Mohawk State Forest closes.

DECEMBER 7, 1941

United States enters World War II after the Japanese attack of Pearl Harbor in Hawaii. Peg Moss enlists as an army nurse in 1942 and Walt in the U.S. Marine Corps in 1944.

1945

World War II ends, first with the surrender of Germany in May and then in August by Japan after the atomic bombings of Hiroshima and Nagasaki.

MID- TO LATE 1940s

American, British and Canadian aviation engineers test de-icing equipment on airplanes. Early successful testing of water nozzles generates freezing rain, fog and sleet conditions. Output from nozzles is described in aviation papers as "snow."

The Guinness Book of World Records later credits Canadian engineer Ray Wringer and colleagues with making the first artificial snow. "They produced so much snow the wind tunnel and engine had to be regularly shut off in order to clear away the snow," the book stated. "Uninterested in pursuing a commercial application, Ringer published his results in the scientific community."

1946

After serving stateside in the Marine Corps as an aerial photographer, Walt Schoenknecht returns to Connecticut. Peg Moss, who served in the Pacific Theater, also returns. Walt and Peg later marry.

OCTOBER 2, 1946

In search of a location for a future ski area, Walt Schoenknecht hikes up Mount Pisgah in West Dover, Vermont. He recalled years later, "I looked down at the snow at my feet—October snow, eighteen inches deep. I looked out at that broad and beautiful valley falling away below me. And most of all, I looked far off into the future. And there, just waiting for me, I saw the ski resort of my dreams."

Winter 1946–47

Newlyweds Walt and Peg Schoenknecht operate a small rope tow area at Brodie Mountain in northwestern Massachusetts. Schoenknecht also meets with Connecticut officials eager to establish the state's first large ski area.

March 1947

Connecticut governor James L. McConaughy, of Cornwall, signs a State Park and Forest Commission lease giving Walt Schoenknecht permission to develop a ski area on Mohawk's northwest slope, known as the Pinnacle. The lease fee for one hundred acres is $100 per year.

March 16, 1947

Last state ski championship race on Mohawk trail that requires a walk up the mountain.

Early 1947

With the help of local ski clubs, the Schoenknecht family begins work on the ski area. An eighteen-ton bulldozer rips out tree stumps and boulders to clear ski trails. The cost of work to open Mohawk was $45,000.

Three engineers leave Chance Voight aircraft company to form the Tey Manufacturing Company of Milford, Connecticut.

November 30, 1947

Article appears in the *Bridgeport Post* with the headlines "State's Snow-Bowl a Skiers' Paradise" and "Winter Wonderland Created in the Mohawk State Forest." Reporter writes that new Pine Lodge is "a mighty fancy one, built of varied-colored masonry blocks, a sky-blue roof, snuggled under a grove of white pine like a remote, Alpine chalet." Inside the lodge is a "food-bar," ski rental/repair shop, toilets and a "baby pen" that holds kids while parents ski. The lodge also serves as home of the Schoenknechts.

December 9, 1947

Walt and Peg Schoenknecht's daughter, Carol, is born. She would later co-own and serve as Mohawk's president well into the twenty-first century.

December 26, 1947

Mohawk Mountain ski area officially opens. It offers six trails, three slopes and six rope tows. Lift passes cost $2 and $1.50 for a half day. During its first day, snow begins to fall—the beginning of a major storm that would bring the most snow seen in some areas since the Blizzard of 1888.

December 28, 1947

Drawn by fresh snow, more than 1,200 skiers show up, including busloads of ski club members.

Late March 1948

Schoenknecht says that he "had wonderful luck" in Mohawk's first season. "A winter like this probably won't come again in years. We might as well be realistic about this." He turned out to be correct.

Fall 1948

Three engineers from the Tey Manufacturing Company of Milford, Connecticut, advertise the ALU-60, an aluminum ski with a hollow interior and three layers of metal. Few people buy the skis because of a nearly snowless winter.

October 6, 1948

Mohawk announces two new trails for its second ski season. The Boulder Bowl area has wide Timber and Wildwood trails with a five-hundred-foot vertical drop and a thirty-degree maximum grade. The trails are served by two tandem rope tows. Also new is the beginner Laurel slope. Parking capacity is doubled to six hundred vehicles.

The 1948–49 ski season has less snow than the previous winter. Most snow comes in early February and mid-March.

December 1949

"Under a shroud of secrecy, in December 1949, Tey brought one of their first snowmaking prototypes to Mohawk Mountain and produced the first documented machine-made snow for skiing," according to a May 1980 article by Nils Ericken in *Ski Area Management* magazine.

December 1949 (*continued*)

Months before his death, Schoenknecht writes, "All this started because snowmaking was born here at Mohawk in 1949."

SKI Magazine also credits Schoenknecht, and the Tey engineers, in 1949 for firing up at Mohawk "a rudimentary snowmaking system on its slopes for the first time."

January 18–21, 1950

Walt Schoenknecht purchases seven hundred tons of ice blocks and, over a two-day period, uses a large chipper to crush it into a skiable surface. The "snow" was spread on the Pinnacle trail and Pine slope. "It was a great idea," Schoenknecht said. "We attracted a great crowd for that weekend's cake walk. But we had to give it up. It turned warm in two days. The ice melted. It was like water going down the drain. The experiment was too expensive to try again."

March 15, 1950

First public announcement of a successful snowmaking machine makes front-page news in newspapers and on a national radio broadcast. Tey president Art Hunt says the machine can make large quantities of snow, "not just handfuls." Hunt, a former Chance Voight aviation engineer, says, "To the best of my knowledge we are the first to convert water to snow in an open field."

October 1950

Schoenknecht tries alternatives to snow; uses pine needles and hay to offer skiing at a Connecticut Ski Council meeting. The bottoms of the skis are covered with a mixture of kerosene and paraffin to increase speed on the trail.

1950–51 ski season

Tey installs two temporary snowmaking systems, first at Mohawk Mountain in Cornwall, Connecticut, and the other at Split Rock Lodge (now Big Boulder) in Pennsylvania's Poconos Mountains.

Fall–Winter 1950

Brothers Joe and Phil Tropeano of Larchmont Farms Company in Lexington, Massachusetts, provide aluminum water piping and related irrigation equipment for Mohawk's first snowmaking system. The Tropeanos develop a water/steam system to produce a mist to protect Florida citrus crops from freezing. They suggest to Tey that the irrigation nozzle used in Florida could be modified to produce snow.

December 13, 1950
Tey requests an irrigation nozzle from Larchmont.

December 14, 1950
Wayne Pierce of the Tey Manufacturing Company applies for U.S. patent on "the method for making snow and distributing snow."

December 28, 1950
Snowmaking system at Mohawk is tested, but "ended inconclusively when below zero cold froze feed lines of the device after only a small amount of snow was produced."

December 30, 1950
Schoenknecht announces that three snowmaking machines now provide "excellent snow conditions."

January 1951
Schoenknecht announces the end of a long testing period for the snowmaking machine developed by Tey. "Successful experiments carried out over the long New Year weekend added almost three inches of man-made snow to an eight-inch packed base."

Mid-January 1951
Warm temperatures stop snowmaking at Mohawk until later in the month.

January 26, 1951
Schoenknecht continues to spread the word about the new snowmaking machine. A ski column in the *Herald News* of Passaic, New Jersey, reports that "his group is working hard on making enough snow for skiers." The column notes, "Mohawk is presently the only ski resort area in New England that is using the Tey snow making machine. The skier will find that the machine, which pumps water into pipes and forces it out of minute holes, makes a beautiful type of corn snow."

DECEMBER 21, 1951

Schoenknecht reports that hundreds of tons of hay that were spread over the ski area last fall resulted in a minimum amount of snow needed for good skiing.

1951

Tey Manufacturing Company merges with Maxwell Equipment Corporation to form Skyworker Corporation to create the first aerial bucket trucks for utility linemen and tree cutting.

OCTOBER 5, 1952

Mohawk hosts the Connecticut Ski Council outing with a hay skiing party on the Boulder Bowl slope. Those wishing to take part in the hay skiing are told to bring ski boots and "beat-up" pair of skis.

DATE UNCERTAIN

When lift lines are long, Walt Schoenknecht starts giving out free cookies and later brownies. Even during his last season at Mohawk, he arranged for the Yale Alley Cats a cappella group to perform outdoors in February 1987. "If you give skiers what they want, they'll come back," he said at the time.

1952–53 SKI SEASON

Directed by Tey engineers, first commercial snowmaking system is installed at Grossinger Hotel in Liberty, New York.

APRIL 27, 1954

Tey's Wayne Pierce is awarded a patent for a snowmaking machine.

DECEMBER 12, 1954

Walt Schoenknecht opens the Mount Snow ski area in West Dover, Vermont. He calls Mohawk Mountain "the mother of Mount Snow." It opens with two chairlifts, two rope tows, seven trails and a base lodge.

1954–55

It's another poor snow year for Mohawk; natural snow finally arrives in March.

1956

Tey Manufacturing Company, now Skyworker Corporation, is sold to Emhart Corporation of Hartford, Connecticut. Art Hunt, the company's former president, notes, "We could see the equipment needed to coat ski slopes would have to be tremendous in size and extremely costly and sold the company and patents."

1956–57

Snowmaking expands to other U.S. ski areas, including Boyne Mountain in Michigan; Bousquet in Pittsfield, Massachusetts; and Laurel Mountain Slopes in Pennsylvania.

1958

Larchmont Engineering announces the company has built a "real snowmaker machine."

1958–59

Eastern Ski Area Directory lists 18 of 104 ski areas in New England and New York that have snowmaking systems.

1959

Larchmont Engineering buys the snowmaking patent from Emhart Corporation.

1960s

Larchmont begins to sue other manufacturers of snowmaking systems. The patent is contested on the basis that Canadian research on making snow had proceeded before Pierce was granted the patent. Tey's patent was overturned on the basis of research by Canadian engineer Ray Ringer in mid- to late 1940s.

1960–61

Mohawk installs first chairlifts at the Boulder Bowl and on the Mohawk trail.

1962

Walt Schoenknecht says that an atomic bomb could be used at Mount Snow to increase the vertical drop at the area's North Face. "The underground blast in the Nevada desert last summer was almost tailor-made for what we need here." The A-bomb plan never happened.

1964

140 ski areas in eastern U.S. and Canada have some type of snowmaking system.

1964–65 SEASON

Mohawk Mountain gets increased competition from other Connecticut ski areas. Areas include Powder Hill (now Powder Ridge Mountain Resort) in Middlefield, Satan's Ridge (now Ski Sundown) in New Hartford, Tapawingo in Woodbury, Mount Hope in Mansfield and the Brooklyn ski area in eastern Connecticut. Mohawk's new base lodge opens. The lodge is styled after the Sun Lodge at Mount Snow in Vermont. Mohawk adds Nutmeg chairlift on wider beginner slope.

1968

Carol Lugar, Walt and Peg's daughter, returns to the East after working for a few years in Vail, Colorado. She would work at Mount Snow as a marketing director and later at Mohawk Mountain as vice-president, co-owner and president.

1969–70

Arrowhead double chairlift is added.

JANUARY 1971

After a series of financial problems and up to $7 million in debt, Walt Schoenknecht sells Mount Snow to Davos Corporation, a processor of specialty meats, seafood and prime beef and owner of a small Catskills, New York ski area. While he remains as Mount Snow president, his role steadily diminishes.

1973

Mohawk sees an uptick in close-to-home customers during the gasoline shortage. Mount Snow vows to gives out-of-state skiers gasoline at its own service station.

1975–76

Mohawk doubles its snowmaking capacity with a new underground six-inch water main to summit. A second, larger pump allows Mohawk to make snow with two different systems. Mohawk general manager Steve Hedden says that "snowmaking was a hobby five years ago; now it's do or die."

AUGUST 1977

The Sherburne Corporation—owners of the Killington ski area in Vermont—purchases Mount Snow for $4.5 million. Killington founder Preston L. Smith once worked with Mohawk's ski patrol.

1978–79 SEASON

With the help of a Sikorsky helicopter, eighteen lift towers are set in place for Mohawk's Boulder triple chair.

1979

Walt Schoenknecht is inducted into the U.S. Ski and Snowboard Hall of Fame. Warm temperatures and lack of natural snow cause Mohawk to open on December 22, about three weeks later than usual.

1982–83

Mohawk reaches 90 percent snowmaking coverage.

MAY 7, 1985

Wayne Pierce, the chief designer of the world's first patented snowmaking machine for a ski area, dies at age sixty-nine. He is buried at the Orange Center Cemetery in Orange, Connecticut.

1985–86

Deer Run chairlift is added.

JANUARY 1986

Schoenknecht signs a thirty-year, renewable lease with the state for use of Mohawk Mountain forestland.

OCTOBER 30, 1987

Walt Schoenknecht dies of prostate cancer at age sixty-eight. Months before his death, he sends a handwritten letter to local ski writers saying, "We're going to make snow come hell or high water." Walt is buried at East Lawn Cemetery in East Haven, Connecticut.

JULY 10, 1989

Tornados ravage Mohawk Mountain, causing $2.5 million in damage to buildings, ski lifts and infrastructure. Tall pine trees at Mohawk and the nearby Cathedral Pines are toppled by strong winds. After the tornado,

Peg Schoenknecht offers her daughter, Carol Lugar, her shares of Mohawk Mountain.

November 24, 1989

Mohawk reopens for the ski season after tornado damage. Mohawk president Carol Lugar says, "It was probably a 15-, 18-year struggle for us to completely come out from under the tornado damage."

1990

Original Pine Lodge, built in 1947, reopens. It was damaged from the 1989 tornado.

July 1991

Mohawk sues American Home Insurance over weather-related policy that stated it would pay $650,000 "per occurrence." Mohawk contends that there were two tornados, not one.

1991–92

After state's approval, Mohawk adds night skiing, increasing business by about 25 percent.

December 15, 1994

Jury rules in favor of Mohawk Mountain, awards an additional $650,000, plus 10 percent interest for the tornado damage.

May 1995

As a way to raise needed cash, Mohawk offers a $1,750 "Gold Pass," for ten years of unlimited skiing.

July 29, 2008

Peg Schoenknecht dies at age ninety.

2008–9

Mohawk triple chairlift is installed.

2013–14

Arrowhead triple chairlift is added.

2015

An 1,800-square-foot addition doubles seating inside Mohawk's main ski lodge.

JANUARY 2017

New thirty-year lease with state begins; covers 244 acres of Mohawk State Forest.

2019–20

Snow tubing is added at Mohawk Mountain.

2023

The National Ski Areas Association says that about 87 percent of its U.S. ski resorts have snowmaking.

BIBLIOGRAPHY

The Mountain, the Land and the People

Clarke, Harriet Lydia, and Andrew Pikosky. *History of East Cornwall*. Cornwall, CT: Cornwall Historical Society, 1977.

Coleman, Margaret. *The Geologic History of Connecticut's Bedrock*. Hartford: Connecticut Department of Environmental Protection, 2005.

Connecticut Forest and Park Association. Pamphlet on CCC ski trails at Mohawk, 1937.

Cornwall Historical Society. "Cathedral Pines." https://cornwallhistoricalsociety. org/cathedral-pines.

———. "Golds Pines." https://cornwallhistoricalsociety.org/golds-pines.

Cudworth, Keith. *The White Memorial Foundation: The First 100 Years*. Litchfield, CT: White Memorial Foundation, 2016.

DeForest, John W. *History of the Indians of Connecticut: From the Earliest Known Period to 1850*. Hartford: Connecticut Historical Society, 1851.

Ericksen, Nils. "A Short History of Snowmaking." *Ski Area Management* (May 1980).

Falles, Edward. *Arsenal of the Revolution*. Salisbury, CT: Lakeview Journal and Tri Corners History Council, 1976.

Gannett, Michael R. *A Historical Guide to the West Cornwall Covered Bridge*. Cornwall, CT: Cornwall Historical Society, 1988.

Horn, Huston. "Vermont's Phenomenal Snowman." *Sports Illustrated* (March 10, 1961).

Hoyt, Joseph. *The Connecticut Story*. New Haven, CT: Readers Press, 1961.

Lavin, Lucianne. *Connecticut's Indigenous Peoples*. New Haven, CT: Yale University Press, 2015.

Life. "Scamp of the Slope" (February 8, 1963): 93–94.

Lorentz, Karen. *Killington: A Story of Mountains and Men.* Shrewsbury, VT: Mountain Publishing Inc., 1990.

Mashantucket Pequot Tribal Nation. "The Pequot War." 2024. https://www.mptn-nsn.gov/pequotwar.aspx.

New Hartford (CT) Tribune. "How Mohawk Mountain Got Its Name." January 20, 1882. https://www.newspapers.com/image/638321361/?match=1&terms=New%20Hartford%20Tribune.

New Haven Ski Club. "History." https://www.newhavenskiclub.com/about.html.

Podskoch, Martin. *Connecticut's Civilian Conservation Corps Camps: History, Memories & Legacy of the CCC.* East Hampton, CT: Podskoch Press, 2016.

Roger Williams National Memorial, Providence, Rhode Island. "King Philip's War (1675–1678)." 2021. https://www.nps.gov/rowi/learn/historyculture/kingphilip.htm.

Rossano, Geoffrey. "Historical and Architectural and Resource Survey of Cornwall, Conn." 2000. https://cornwallhistoricalsociety.org/wp-content/uploads/2023/03/Historic-and-Architectural-Cornwall-Book-2-23-COPY.pdf.

Salisbury Cannon Museum. "About Ethan Allen." http://www.salisburycannonmuseum.org.

Sportman, Sarah P. "Connecticut at the Ends of the Last Ice Age: The Farmington Mastodon and the First Human Settlers." White Memorial Conservation Center. https://whitememorialcc.org/wp-content/uploads/2020/12/Winter-Newsletter-2021.pdf.

Stone, Timothy. *Cornwall and Its Ancient Settlers.* Cornwall, CT: Cornwall Historical Society, 1999.

Works Progress Administration. *Connecticut: A Guide to Its Roads, Lore, and People.* Boston: Houghton Mifflin Company, 1938.

The Beginning of the Mohawk Mountain Ski Area

American Lung Association. "State of the Air: Report Card Connecticut." https://www.lung.org/research/sota/city-rankings/states/connecticut.

Audubon Connecticut. "Important Bird Areas: White Memorial Foundation." https://ct.audubon.org/conservation/white-memorial-foundation.

Britton, R.D. "Along the Ski Trails." *Hartford Courant,* January 21, 1942.

Clarke, Harriet L. *Mohawk Towers.* Cornwall, CT: Cornwall Historical Society, 1988.

Connecticut Department of Energy and Environmental Protection. *Mohawk Mountain State Forest Map Winter Recreation Use.* Map. https://portal.ct.gov/-/media/deep/stateparks/maps/mohawkswinterpdf.pdf.

Connecticut General Assembly. "Civilian Conservation Corps in Connecticut." 1999. https://www.cga.ct.gov/PS99/rpt%5Colr%5Chtm/99-R-0955.htm.

Cornwall Historical Society. "Colliers and the Iron Industry." https://
    cornwallhistoricalsociety.org/colliers-and-the-iron-industry.
Cudworth, Keith. *The White Memorial Foundation: The First 100 Years.* Litchfield, CT:
    White Memorial Foundation, 2016.
Podskoch, Martin. *Connecticut's Civilian Conservation Corps Camps: History, Memories &
    Legacy of the CCC.* East Hampton, CT: Podskoch Press, 2016.
Works Progress Administration. *Connecticut: A Guide to Its Roads, Lore, and People.*
    Boston: Houghton Mifflin Company, 1938.

Mohawk Mountain's First Ski Season

Bridgeport (CT) Sunday Post. "State's Snow-Bowl a Skiers' Paradise." November 30,
    1947.
Davis, Jeremy. "Lost Ski Areas in Connecticut." New England Lost Ski Area
    Project. https://www.nelsap.org/ct/ct.html.
The Day (New London, CT). "Blizzard Brings 12 to 20 Inches of Snow."
    December 27, 1947.
———. "Ski Conditions Reported in State Forests." January 5, 1946.
Hartford Courant. "Mohawk Mountain's First Ski Season." January 2, 1948.
———. "Ski Areas within 150 Miles from Hartford." December 26, 1947.
Hartford Times. "New Area of Mohawk Mountain Opens for Its Second Season."
    October 6, 1948.
Litchfield (CT) Enquirer. "Walt Schoenknecht: Mohawk Mountain Ski Area Location
    Took Years of Study." December 1947.
Lugar, Carol (Schoenknecht). Phone interview, May 8, 2024.
Maloney, Ken. "Ski Trail." *Bridgeport (CT) Post,* January 29, 1970.
New Haven Register. "East Havener Walt Schoenknecht Banks Future on Snow-
    Covered Slops of Mohawk Mountain." February 15, 1953.
New Haven Ski Club. "History." https://newhavenskiclub.com/about.
    html#:~:text=and%20rich%20history.-,Club%20History,Club%20and%20
    Yale%20Golf%20Course.
New York Times. Robert E. Moss, obituary, April 24, 1964. https://www.nytimes.
    com/1964/04/24/archives/robert-f-moss-exsteel-official-engineer-who-led-
    concern-in-tokyo.html.
Stevens, Richard A. "Brief Baedecker for Connecticut Skiers." *Hartford Courant
    Magazine* (December 21, 1947).
Teague, Wendell A. "Berkshire Is Attractive to Conn. Skiers." *Hartford Daily
    Courant,* December 30. 1938.
Whitman, Royal. "Early Review of New Mohawk Mountain Ski Area." *Hartford
    Times,* November 26, 1947.

Birth of Snowmaking: Disappointments and, Finally, Success

American Ski Annual and Skiing Journal. "How Crushed Ice Saved the Weekend at Mohawk Mountain" (1950–51).

Associated Press. "Engineers Have a Way to Coat Hills with Artificial Snow." March 16, 1950.

———. "Ski Tow Patron, Hurt in Cornwall Loses Damage Suit." December 15, 1950.

Bellis, Mary. "Making Snow." The Inventors. https://theinventors.org/library/inventors/blsnow.htm.

Berry, I. William. *The Great North American Ski Book.* New York: Charles Scribner's Sons, 1984.

Blaisdell, Harold F. "Pipe the Snow." *American Ski Annual and Skiing Journal* (1952): 69.

Boston Herald. "Garden Show Holding Sports Spotlight as N.E. Waits Real Snow." December 3, 1937.

Bridgeport (CT) *Sunday Herald.* "Mohawk Trail to Use Artificial Snow Whenever Nature Fails." December 10, 1950.

Eastern Skier Magazine. "Snow Making Is 'Practical' $25,000 Air-Water Sprayer Network Operates Successfully at Mohawk" (January 15, 1951).

Ericksen, Nils. "A Short History of Snowmaking." *Ski Area Management* (May 1980).

Guinness Book of World Records. "First Artificial Snow." https://www.guinnessworldrecords.com/world-records/383275-first-artificial-snow.

Hall, Fred A. *Manufacturing Snow by Shaving.* Montreal: Canadian Ski Year Book, 1934.

Hardy, Pat. "Man Makes Snow!!!" *Boston Globe*, March 16, 1950.

Hartford Courant. Alling Rubber Company ski equipment ad, October 10, 1948.

———. J.R. Hobson, patent lawyer and Emhart officer, obituary, May 19, 1994. https://www.courant.com/1994/05/19/john-robert-hobson-was-officer-at-emhart-mountain-climber-2.

———. "Snow-Making Machine Still in the Experimental Stage." December 15, 1950.

Hunt, Arthur R. "Snowmaking Is 40 Years Old." *Ski Area Management* (March 1990).

Iowa Nonpareil (Council Bluffs). "Snow-Making Machine Capable of Turning Out Eight Tons of Snow in 24 Hours." March 7, 1949.

LeCompte, Tom. "Snow-Making Inventors Earn Next to Nothing, Sell Company." *American Ski Annual and Skiing Journal* (Winter 2007): 34–35.

Lugar, Carol (Schoenknecht). Interview, May 8, 2024.

National Skiing 7, no. 6. "St. Peter's Helpers" (January 15, 1955): 14.

New England Ski Museum. "Chronology of Snowmaking." https://newenglandskimuseum.org/wp-content/uploads/2012/06/snowmaking_timeline.pdf.

New Haven Register. "East Havener Walt Schoenknecht Banks Future on Snow-Covered Slopes of Mohawk Mountain." February 15, 1953.

New York Daily News. "The Iceman Cometh." Five photos of Mohawk's crushed ice skiing run on the back page, January 23, 1950.

New York Times. "Making Artificial Snow for Connecticut Skiers." January 29, 1950.

Pesko, Walter, and Dorothy Nadler. "Artificial Clouds and Pine Needles Among Varied Plans of Walt Schoenknecht of Mohawk Mountain Ski Area." *Hartford Courant Magazine* (October 22, 1950).

South Coast Times (Australia). "Artificial Snow for U.S. Skiers." May 22, 1950.

Union Leader. William Walsh, snowmaking pioneer and Connecticut native, obituary. https://www.legacy.com/us/obituaries/unionleader/name/william-walsh-obituary?id=52137586#:~:text=William%20Arthur%20Walsh%2C%20 Jr%2C%20BS,around%20his%20family%20and%20career.

Mohawk Founder Opens Mount Snow in Vermont

Bennington Banner. "Atomic Blasting in Vermont?" Editorial, January 19, 1963.

Berkshire Eagle. "New Stowe Lift Dedicated; Mount Snow Starts Running." December 20, 1954.

Berry, I. William. *The Great North American Ski Book*. New York: Charles Scribner's Sons, 1984, 51–52.

Birmingham, Dot. "Will Skiing Jump Off the Deep End?: West Hartford Designer Predicts Less Skiing, More Socializing, Plastic Snow and Resort-Lodges." *Hartford Courant*, February 26, 1967.

Brattleboro Reformer. "Auto Crashes, Near Riot Give Mount Snow Worries." March 5, 1956.

———. "The Pains of Success." March 7, 1956.

Cuyler, Lew. "A Visit with Mt. Snow's Walt Schoenkencht." *North Adams Transcript*, February 16, 1974.

Fry, John. *The Story of Modern Skiing*. Lebanon, NH: University Press of New England, 2006, 47, 49, 51–56, 65.

Holloway, Grady. "Mt. Snow to Be Schoenknechted into 40,000-Skiers-a-Day Vermont Fun City?" *Bennington Banner*, March 16, 1970.

Hooper, John S. "Man, Mountain and Money." *Brattleboro Reformer*, December 21, 1968.

Horn, Houston. "Vermont's Phenomenal Snowman." *Sports Illustrated* (March 20, 1961).

Kull, Nell M. *History of Dover, Vermont: 100 Years in a Hill Town*. Brattleboro, VT: Book Seller, 1961.

LIFE. "The Scamp of the Slope." February 8, 1963, 93–94.

Lugar, Carol (Schoenknecht). Interview, May 8, 2024.

Official Highway Map of Vermont—The Green Mountain State. Vermont Department of Highways and Vermont Development Commission road map, 1954–55.

Pesko, Walt, and Artie Donovan. "Schoenknecht Duet." *Hartford Courant,* December 3, 1953.

Rutland Herald. "Skiing Aids Economy." September 6, 1961.

Stein, Pinky. "Life Line." *Holyoke (MA) Transcript,* March 8, 1974.

Vander Voort, John, and John Hitchcock. "New Mount Snow Ski Area to Have Two Chairlifts Running This Year." *Berkshire Eagle,* October 13, 1954.

Vermont Board of Agriculture. Pamphlet on state's resources and home for sale, 1892.

Vermont Public. "Mount Snow: The First 40 Years." 1994. https://www.youtube.com/watch?v=mNaGkZ0c43Q&t=259s.

Tornados Ravage Mohawk Mountain

Cornwall Historical Society. "1989 Tornado." https://cornwallhistoricalsociety.org/1989-tornado.

Hanrahan, Ryan. "The 1989 Tornado Outbreak." https://ryanhanrahan.substack.com/p/the-1989-tornado-outbreak.

Hartford Courant. "Skiing to Resume at Mohawk Mountain." November 20, 1989.

Longley, Robert. "Night Skiing Plan Gets Cold Shoulder." *Lakeville Journal,* September 5, 1991.

Lugar, Carol (Schoenknecht), and Steve Hedden. Interview, April 11, 2024.

Meriden Journal-Record. "Family Bought Cathedral Pines Mourn Their Loss." July 23, 1989.

Mohawk Mountain Ski Area. "$1,750 'Gold Pass.'" Press release, May 1995.

National Oceanic and Atmospheric Administration database. Litchfield County, July 10, 1989 tornados. https://www.ncdc.noaa.gov/stormevents/eventdetails.jsp?id=9985068.

———. New Haven County, July 10, 1989 tornados. https://www.ncdc.noaa.gov/stormevents/eventdetails.jsp?id=9985073.

National Oceanic and Atmospheric Administration. "Enhanced Fujita Scale." https://www.weather.gov/oun/efscale.

———. "Fujita Scale." https://www.spc.noaa.gov/faq/tornado/f-scale.html.

Pane, Lisa Marie. "Officials Optimistic on Repairs to Storm-Damaged Slopes." *Hartford Courant,* August 31, 1989.

Pruitt, Gail. "Number of Tornadoes Key to Mohawk Mountain's Lawsuit Over Insurance." *Hartford Courant,* July 20, 1991.

Rowan, David. "Tornado!" *Ski Area Management* (September 1989).

Shay, James. "Mohawk Finally Sees the Light with Night Skiing." *Bridgeport Post*, December 1991.

Waller, Ben. Interview on Mohawk tornados, March 10, 2024.

Decades Bring Boom, Bust and More Ski Areas

Canfield, Owen. "Mohawk's a Cold Spot that Can Warm You Up." *Hartford Courant*, February 4, 1997.

Carlson, Barbara. "Ski Resorts Reap Green Stuff with Each Layer of White Stuff." *Hartford Courant*, January 8, 1981.

Fry, John. *The Story of Modern Skiing*. Lebanon, NH: University Press of New England, 2006.

Hartford Courant. "New England Ski Guide." December 6, 1964.

Holroyd, Barbara. "Ski Fever." *Meriden (CT) Journal*, December 19, 1963.

Journal of the New England Ski Museum, no. 12. "Connecticut Ski Areas" (Spring 2019): 4–18.

Kenny, Jerry. "Slant on Skiing." *New York Daily News*, January 23, 1970.

Lakeville Journal. "Mohawk Has Found a New Future." February 2, 1978.

Meriden Journal. "West Rock Proposed for Ski Run." July 27, 1960.

Naugatuck Daily News. "Mohawk Starts a Big Comeback." January 7, 1961.

New England Ski History. "Connecticut." https://www.newenglandskihistory. com/Connecticut.

Shay, James. "Rod Taylor's One-Man Band." *SKI Magazine* (October 1992): E13–15.

U.S. Ski and Snowboard Hall of Fame. "Walt Schoenknecht Inducted into U.S. Ski and Snowboard Hall of Fame." 1979. https://skihall.com/hall-of-famers/ walter-schoenknecht.

Western Daily Express (Bristol, England). "Drug Crisis at Pop Festival that Wasn't." August 3, 1970.

How the Mohawk Ski Area Survives

Dixon, Ken. "With Skis in Hand, Lamont Announces Plan to Expand Offerings in State Parks." *CT Insider*, January 12, 2024.

State of Connecticut. "Mohawk Mountain Ski Area Inc." https://service.ct.gov/ business/s/onlinebusinesssearch?businessNameEn=ZsjWkotKhCG%2BGo%2 BaQ%2BIuJwYbXEd9QaAaT8oZy9EksGXWSe8IIGcV7X9F3jpkoZ5T.

TechnoAlpin. "Snow Guns for Extensive Snow Coverage." https://www. technoalpin.com/en/snow-guns/fan-guns.

Wallis, Harriett. "Mohawk Mountain a Friendly Place to Ski." *Journal Inquirer* (Manchester, CT), January 22, 1987.

ABOUT THE AUTHOR

James Shay's first experience skiing was about fifty years ago, when he went to the top of Vermont's Killington Peak and fell more than twenty times on the way down. Shortly afterward, he enrolled in a ski school in St. Anton, Austria, and has been skiing ever since. A journalist for more than forty years, he got his first reporting job at the local newspaper, where he would meet his future wife. He retired from Hearst Connecticut Media in 2021. His snow sports writing has appeared in *SKI Magazine*, *Snow Country*, national/regional ski guides and on digital news sites. He has skied in the Alps, the Rocky Mountains, from New Mexico to British Columbia, most areas in the Northeast and, of course, Mohawk Mountain.